OUR CHIEFS AND ELDERS

OUR CHIEFS

DAVID NEEL

AND ELDERS]

Words and Photographs

of Native Leaders

UBC Press / Vancouver
University of Washington Press / Seattle

© UBC Press 1992

All rights reserved

ISBN 0-7748-0411-4

Canadian Cataloguing in Publication Data

Neel, David.
    Our chiefs and elders

    Includes bibliographical references.
    ISBN 0-7748-0411-4

    1. Indians of North America – British Columbia –
Interviews. 2. Indians of North America – British Columbia –
Portraits. I. Title.
E78.B9N43 1992   971.1'00497   C92-091574-4

*Publication of this book was made possible by ongoing support from
The Canada Council, the Province of British Columbia Cultural
Services Branch, and the Department of Communications of the
Government of Canada. ¶ The book has also been financially as-
sisted by the Province of British Columbia through the British
Columbia Heritage Trust and BC Lottery Fund, and by Multicultu-
ralism and Citizenship Canada.*

UBC Press
University of British Columbia
6344 Memorial Rd
Vancouver, BC V6T 1Z2
(604) 822-3259
Fax: (604) 822-6083

Published simultaneously in the United States of America by
The University of Washington Press, PO Box 50096, Seattle,
Washington 98145-5096

ISBN 0-295-97217-3

Library of Congress Cataloging-in-Publication Data

Neel, David.
    Our chiefs and elders : words and photographs of native
leaders / David Neel.
        p.   cm.
    Includes bibliographical references.
    ISBN 0-295-97217-3

    1. Kwakiutl Indians – Portraits. 2. Kwakiutl Indians –
Social life and customs. 3. Indians of North America –
British Columbia – Portraits. I. Title.
E99.K9N44 1992
971.1'004979 – dc20   92-24652

DEDICATION

To my father, Dave Neel, whose work I continue today.

ACKNOWLEDGMENTS

It is not possible to recognize all the many people who helped in making this book possible, though I would like to mention the support of the following:

Canada Council

Kodak Canada

UBC Museum of Anthropology

Edwin and Vera Newman

Emma Tamlin

Sharon Neel

Steve Ray

The Kwakwaka'wakw People

CONTENTS

FOREWORD

CHIEF ELIJAH HARPER
MLA, RUPERT'S LAND

I AM VERY HONOURED TO INTRODUCE THIS SPLENDID BOOK DEPICTING NATIVE CHIEFS AND ELDERS OF BRITISH COLUMBIA. DAVID NEEL'S WORK HAS RIGHTLY BEEN PRAISED FOR ITS OUTSTANDING QUALITY AND CONTENT, AND THIS BOOK WILL CONFIRM THAT THAT PRAISE IS WELL DESERVED. ¶ THESE PORTRAITS ARE NOT JUST OUTSTANDING BY ANY PHOTOGRAPHIC STANDARD; THEY ARE ALSO SIGNIFICANT BECAUSE THEY BREAK THROUGH THE STEREOTYPES THAT HAVE DOMINATED PORTRAITS OF ABORIGINAL PEOPLE IN NORTH AMERICA. WE HAVE ALWAYS HAD GREAT LEADERS IN OUR COMMUNITIES, BUT RECORDED PORTRAITS IN THE PAST SELDOM REFLECTED THIS FACT. WITH THIS BOOK, FOR THE FIRST TIME, THE LEADERSHIP QUALITIES OF ABORIGINAL PEOPLE ARE SHOWN FOR ALL TO SEE. ¶ EARLIER PUBLIC IMAGES OF ABORIGINAL PEOPLE HAVE BEEN ALMOST COMPLETELY NEGATIVE. IN THIS BOOK OUR LEADERS STEP OUT OF THE MARGINS AND ARE PRESENTED IN TRULY NATURAL SETTINGS. THESE PORTRAITS ARE TRIBUTES TO PEOPLE WHO HAVE INSPIRED OUR COMMUNITIES THROUGHOUT THIS CENTURY. MAY THEY ALSO INSPIRE ALL THOSE WHO READ THIS BOOK.

INTRODUCTION

DAVID NEEL

WHEN I set out to photograph the Native leaders of British Columbia, I was not aware of the effect the experience would have on my life. Four years and three babies later, a book is born. This body of work is intended to be the antithesis of the 'vanishing race' photographs of Native people – this is a statement of the surviving race. It has been my intention to let the people speak for themselves. For this reason the text appears as unedited as possible, as it was told to me between 1988 and 1991. These people serve as the conduits of a knowledge that has come down through time to be handed on into the future. Through their words, it is my hope that you will be able to see beyond the stereotype to the person behind and gain a better understanding of what Aboriginal culture and people are about. History has shown that allowing people to tell their own story is the only way a greater understanding between cultures can occur. The photographs are my interpretation, my vision, of these human beings. I photograph these people as I do all races, striving to go behind the physical appearance to show the humanness of, or common thread between, people.

This, it seems to me, is of particular importance at this time, as the Native and non-Native nations work toward setting aside the errors of the past to define a new relationship. It seems fitting that the words of our leaders should add to the process of understanding at this time, the quincentennial of the discovery of Christopher Columbus by Native Americans. It seems so basic, in searching for knowledge about a people, to talk to the leadership. The elders tell us that we need to know the past to understand our present and future. The time has come for the First Nations to speak for ourselves and to create our own images. And who knows better than our leaders what those images are? ¶ My photography has been influenced by the 'concerned photographers,' such as Cartier Bresson, Cornell Capa, and W. Eugene Smith. These are men idealistic enough to believe that photographs can make a difference – that they can help humanity understand itself. I would like to believe this myself, but what I feel is hope rather than belief. Certainly photographs greatly influence our understanding of the world, so it is important that there are photographers working to illustrate what they see as the truth. Perhaps my biggest influence has been W. Eugene Smith, the *Life* magazine photographer and father of the photo-essay. He told the story of many people, including that of the people of Minamata, Japan, and their struggle with industrially induced mercury poisoning. Unfortunately, like many great artists, he died poor, with a great talent and an incredible body of work. I greatly admire people, like Smith, who stand for what they believe through times of trial. An artist or photographer needs that strength of vision to see him or her through the difficult periods. Another major influence on my work was provided by Irving Penn, an artist and commercial photographer whose technique is brilliant. His 'Worlds in a Small Room' approach has an obvious influence on my work, although I take a 180° turn from him with respect to how I approach my subject. His images are impersonal, crafted for immediate impact, and illuminate the strangeness of the sitter. This is the approach of much of the magazine photography we see today. I, on the other hand, strive to photograph that which is common between us, though a person may look and dress quite differently from you or I. ¶ As I set out to photograph the chiefs and elders, I thought that I would be seeking out the oldest and the wisest. As I met people, it became clear that each had a contribution to make. Like chapters in a book, they come together to tell

a story. Research and selection was carried out through word of mouth – what anthropologists used to call 'informants' and 'fieldwork.' By talking to people I would be led from one person to the next. When I planned to visit an area I would talk to one or two acquaintances from that village or tribe and get a name or two. I invariably found my way to someone who became a 'chapter' in this book. I feel that the selection of people included in this collection constitutes a reasonable representation of Northwest Coast elders – at least insofar as any group of fifty or so people could. In hindsight, it seems as though I was being led to the people I needed to meet with. Like the process of photography, this seems extraordinary. ¶ When I photograph people I set up my equipment, we talk, I take pictures, and it is a relaxed, shared experience. When the photographs are developed, and one selected, a visual statement about that person and their life is the result. I have never understood the process at an intellectual level – it is more a matter of intuition – and I've simply come to trust it. Photography, at its best, can go behind the physical self to reflect a person's soul on a piece of sensitized paper. When it works, it is magical – and the longer I take pictures the more often the magic works. I approach photography as a personal vision. What the pictures say, to some degree, embodies what I choose to say about the person and what I feel about him or her. Photographs are not objective. Once this is recognized, one can see a portrait for what it is – a result of an interaction between two people. A photo session is a sharing experience – I try to share with my subjects, as they share with me, the resulting image. I have made an effort to have these images project truthful representations of the leaders. I am aware that photographs live on beyond the subjects or photographer, and it is my hope that these will be found to be fair representations as time moves on and they become a part of history. ¶ In an effort to show the people in their fullness, as individuals, I have photographed them in a variety of activities and settings. Native people are and do many things. Everything shown is real – a part of their lives. The ceremonial regalia, depicting crests and lineages, are owned and used by the subjects. I have tried to show the people as they are, with their lives in two worlds, two cultures. While they may live in modern homes, drive automobiles, and attend rallies in the city, they tenaciously hang on to their traditional ways and values. Whether you fish in a canoe or a gas boat, or carve totem poles with metal or stone tools, is not the issue. Indigenous people have a place in contemporary society, and their traditional culture has come with them. These photographs strive to illustrate this. ¶ I learned much while talking to the chiefs and elders. In part

it was a process of self-discovery and education. I was born into a family with a long history in Kwagiutl art. My father and grandmother, both artists, I lost in my childhood and so was raised by my mother in Alberta, away from my father's culture and people. During this time, my mother taught me to stand on my own feet – to be self-sufficient. Later, my elders spoke to me of the importance of self-sufficiency. After living and travelling in Canada, the United States, and Mexico, I returned home, an adult and a photographer, to see the Coast with new eyes. Upon my return, I was intensely curious about my culture and heritage and sought to continue the social/documentary photography, in addition to the commercial work, I had been doing in the United States. It was two years before I had a vision of what I felt I wanted to do. It seemed obvious that the elders and chiefs were the foundation, and I began to seek them out. This project, undertaken in my late twenties, was to be my education, my 'master's degree,' in my culture. As is the case with learning, what I learned was how much there is to know, and how little of it I know. It made me long for the time of my grandparents, when extended families were close (four to six families sharing a bighouse) and were headed by an elder or elders who daily passed on age-old knowledge. As we learn from our elders, we find it's not necessary to reinvent the wheel in our youth. Inherited knowledge allows us to learn from the mistakes of previous generations. ¶ I came to mourn what had been lost as well as to take joy in how much remained. The elders of this generation will be the last to witness the time before cars and gas boats. Many were born in bighouses, travelled in log canoes, lived from the land, and some still speak only their own Native language. We will not see elders like this again, I am afraid. The roles of elders, hereditary chiefs, elected chief councillors, and youth became known to me. The people shared much with me because I was a young person who wanted to know. This is what is called tradition – the passing on of knowledge to the young who want to know. I came to understand that lifestyle will always change – what is important is that the culture, language, and values be retained. This takes a real effort on the part of the people. Today we are witnessing the rebirth of our cultures on the Northwest Coast. We can see the end of a period of oppression, and we can see a time of hope for our grandchildren. We are entering into a time in which Aboriginal people have a place in contemporary society. The Native has learned much – it is now time that society learn from the Native. ¶ My desire to photograph the leaders began as I slowly came to realize that, for well over a hundred years, we have learned to accept a false image of the people of the First Nations. The tool used to build this

image has been the camera, and the subject has been the 'Native Indian.' This image has not been a kind one, and it has laid the foundation for a century of misunderstanding between Natives and non-Natives. For this reason, the First Nations are realizing the need, and acquiring the skill, to represent ourselves to the world. We live in a time of the created image – if you do not create your own, someone will create it for you. The image created for us is one of a people stuck in time, as though we are not part of the twentieth century. As early as the mid-1800s, Native people were viewed as part of the past and were imagined to be a 'vanishing race.' Cultural evolution is not something in which we are seen to participate. Our history ended with the coming of photography and Hollywood. I have heard people ask many times, 'Are there still Indians today?' When depicted in popular culture, we are either a 'noble savage' or a 'degraded heathen.' Both are one-dimensional stereotypes, which flatten human individuals into created, dehumanized classifications. This treatment is not limited to Native people – just look at your evening newspaper or TV news. But who else has been painted so generally with so broad a stroke? Not that the early photographers, anthropologists, and ethnologists had universally bad intentions. Ethnocentricity and a feeling of cultural superiority were the standard of the day. This colonial mentality colours the image-making of Native people even to this day. ¶ The process of misinformation and colonization was aided by both the arts, such as photography, and by the sciences, such as anthropology. Many of the sciences have been applied toward proving the inferiority of the First Nations. Social Darwinism has been taken to prove that the colonizing nation, or more 'highly evolved' race, has a right to do what it pleases with the First Nations, and that this simply demonstrates the 'survival of the fittest.' The First Nations, according to this position, are, by definition, inferior. Thus human society and relations are reduced to the level of an ant colony. An essential measure of the 'progress' of a society may be defined by how seriously it critiques the colonialist roots by which it obtained its 'original' territory. Colonialism, by nature, sets aside the rights and history of one people for the needs and desires of another – always with disastrous effects. ¶ Photography has been used since the last century to support these ideas of cultural superiority, to the loss of the First Nations of the world. The roots of this ethnocentric attitude began before the popular use of photography. When the tall ships first began to visit North America, artists were present to record and interpret the 'discovered' people. Artists were to produce the first images of Native life and culture for a White audience. The filtered image began its life here – with broad artistic licence being applied. It

was typical for tribal groups, settings, and cultural practices and items to be moved back and forth in order to produce a finished painting. This practice laid the foundation for the approach to contemporary photography in which the desired image is moulded by adding props, deleting signs of contemporary life, and selecting background to correspond to White ideas of the 'authentic' Native person. The goal was not to strive for a fair or accurate depiction but for visual impact, or viewer response, to the image. The manipulated image became the accepted norm, as it continues to be today. The thirst for manipulated photographs, and the diversion from truth, was augmented with the rise in popularity of collecting photographs of 'noble savages.' This market for photographs of 'savages' as curiosities was such that, by the 1880s, a high degree of control in the portrayal of Native subjects was the accepted norm. Today it is still a popular pastime to collect 'Indian photographs,' some of which fetch prices in the thousands. ¶ Most Native photography occurred during a painful period of Native American history. A good deal of omission, selection, and propping was required to mould a publicly acceptable image. There was a market for photographs of the noble savage, not the degraded heathen. Since Native people were, at this time, combining Western clothes, tools, and so on with their own culture, some careful filtering was required to show the 'savage' in his or her most 'primitive' state, as the market dictated. Although the noble savage was the dominant image of the day, there were photographers interested in showing the story of contact and change. Of these the most notable are perhaps Lloyd Winter and Percy Pond of Juneau, Alaska. Although there was a minority of photographers creating truthful images, the romanticized noble savage was the mainstay of the day. ¶ There were many photographers of this genre, but it was Edward S. Curtis who most influenced North American attitudes about Natives. Probably the most well known and prolific of the so-called 'Indian photographers,' Curtis was to take the romantic savage myth one step further into the 'vanishing race' myth. The premise of his work was that North American Natives were a 'vanishing race,' and it was to be his life's work to 'save' them from this abrupt end by capturing them on film. This grand enterprise was undertaken with the endorsement of Theodore Roosevelt and with the $75,000 financial backing of J. Pierpont Morgan. A newspaper headline of the day read, 'Morgan Money to Keep Indians from Oblivion.' The result was *The North American Indian*, a twenty-volume set of photographs and text, which has done more to misinform and shape attitudes toward Native people than the work of any other photographer. When Curtis's photographs are

viewed as art, they are quite wonderful. However, they are very problematic when one starts to examine them for authenticity, integrity, and general content. ¶ The main problem Curtis's images create has to do with the idea of the vanishing race. There was a commonly held belief that the Native people of North America were vanishing and would soon be gone. This was desirable for the time, as the territory they historically occupied was wanted for Caucasian immigration and expansion. Curtis's vanishing race vision became popular following the Indian Wars in the United States. It coincided, approximately, with the potlatch and sundance prohibition era in Canada and the United States and with the flu and smallpox epidemics in various communities. There was active suppression of Native culture and oppression of the people – at a time when there was a public desire for images of 'authentic' pre-contact Natives in their primitive state. At the same time that the culture and people were being systematically uprooted, there was a need for images affirming primitive humanity in touch with the natural world. This was also an era of technological and industrial boom and belief in unlimited growth potential. It was as though the public wanted confirmation of the existence of a frontier – an image of a primitive human, existing like a hunting trophy or a fish in an aquarium. ¶ From this foundation Curtis set out to capture the

Native as he/she existed many years previously. This required some effort and ingenuity, as he got started in approximately 1900, and his vision of the 'primitive' Indian was from 100 to 200 years in the past. He steps outside time to accomplish this, thereby misleading his audience, who thought (and continue to think) that they were seeing how actual, individual people really lived at that time. A very fine photographer, he was nonetheless able to manipulate his images without the encumbrance of professional ethics or conscience. In his quest for his personal vision of authenticity, and to fit the publicly accepted notion of the 'primitive Indian,' he often supplied his subjects with wigs and props. His views of the romantic savage were typical of the times. In addition to using wigs, he has been criticized for dressing subjects in clothing that actually belonged to other tribal groups. This visual cocktail is comparable to photographing a French woman in a traditional Italian dress and offering this as an image of an 'authentic' European. Curtis, as knowledgeable as he was of the vast differences between tribal groups, and even villages, felt free to mix and match as desired. This 'pan-Indian' approach has continued to be the standard for dealing with Native people in popular culture (e.g., Hollywood). ¶ Curtis's tactics for making his photographs did not stop short of lies, bribery, and deception. His unethical and compromising attitude toward his

Native subjects is seen in his 'Sacred Mandan Turtles' photograph. In order to photograph these sacred ritual objects against the wishes of the Mandan people, he bribed a Mandan priest, Packs Wolf. After many months of effort, Packs Wolf 'consented' and told Curtis to come in early winter. Following partaking of a sweatlodge to 'purify' himself, he was able to photograph the sacred objects. However, he was nearly caught and had to pretend to be recording the priest singing in order to cover his actions. Practices of this sort were not unique to Curtis – deception of Native people was common. Even the renowned anthropologist, Franz Boas, was known to use bribery to obtain ritual items against the traditions and wishes of the people. He was also known to rob graves by night, which was a common feature of the anthropology of the day. Today, the remains of thousands of Native people are stored in the archives of the most 'credible' museums and institutions, and this has become a contentious issue, as descendants are rightfully demanding the return of their ancestors' bones. This disrespect was pervasive in the collection of material dealing with Native people. Such actions as grave-robbing were acceptable because anthropology, and other studies associated with Native people, was based on the idea that they were inferior and not deserving of the basic human rights due the Caucasian race. Photography has been used, with a good dose of manipulation, to support this attitude. ¶ It has laid the foundation for the way non-Natives have thought, and continue to think, about Natives. The work of Curtis is good art. His skill in portraying his subjects is timeless – a testament to his abilities as a photographer as well as to his rapport with Native people. Today, there continues to be a lucrative market for photogravures of his photography. However, their popularity with collectors and as illustrations of Native life continues his campaign of misinformation. The vanished race myth lives on. It is unfortunate that Curtis did not at least choose to show the contemporary living conditions of his subjects, in addition to his own misguided vision. ¶ The impact of the 'Indian Photographers' has been large. They have become the visual norm in the popular misunderstanding and depiction of Native people. Today, these photographs are seen on calendars, postcards, and in numerous books. The photographs have become disassociated from their context and are accepted as genuine. They continue to support the vanishing race attitude toward Aboriginal people, perhaps more than ever because of increased circulation and acceptance. What is most disturbing is that these images have come back into our communities to influence how our own people look at our culture and heritage! Due to a lack of understanding, our young people interpret these photographs as accurate depictions of our ancestors

and their way of life. The very sources of public education, our Native cultural centres as well as public museums, distribute this material as authentic ethnography, when they are, at best, loosely based re-creations. The public image of Native people has not been widely modernized since the last century – hence, Native Americans have become vestiges of the past. This attitude has been transplanted to other parts of the globe as well, where it supports similar expansion and resource exploitation. The reality of contemporary Native people and their culture is only now starting to trickle out. ¶ The public has had little opportunity to see why issues like self-government, the land question, and fishing and hunting rights should be connected with a 'vanishing race.' On a recent research trip to the American Museum of Natural History in New York, I heard a museum guide talk about a 'potlatch that was' and 'Indian people that were.' I thought of all the potlatches I have attended in recent years and of all the 'Indians' I know – many of them relatives. What has vanished is the lifestyle – the people remain. We remain as people, as nations, striving to hang on to the valuable parts of a culture handed on to us through our elders. Native people are not vestiges of the past, as much photography leads us to believe. First Nations evolve, as every culture of the world evolves. When a culture stops moving, and ennui sets in, so does decadence.

Native people have been depicted as part of another age because White governments have deemed it convenient to do so. To recognize Native nations would mean recognizing human rights, self-government, and the land question. To acknowledge First Nations would not be consistent with the ban against potlatches between 1884 and 1951, Wounded Knee (1891), or the Gitksan/Wet'suet'en decision (1991). This dichotomy has served White society well. As we of the First Nations are learning to speak for ourselves, it is becoming increasingly difficult to believe in the images of the past. ¶ We are learning to use the tools of contemporary society, in some cases the very tools that have been used against us. Until the middle of this century, we did not have a right to hire lawyers, raise funds for the pursuit of legal cases, or even to exercise the federal vote. Today, these and other tools are being used to improve our lives. During the constitutional amendments of the 1970s, the Native people of Canada had little direct political redress when their concerns were overlooked. In the constitutional accord of the 1990s, we were to see an elected Native MP stop the Meech Lake Accord, when, once again, we were left out. In British Columbia, we are witnessing negotiations and modern-day treaties being undertaken by tribal, federal, and provincial governments. The courts have become the arena for settling long-standing issues such as the land question. Some of these cases are multi-million dollar affairs, encompassing years of research and extensive legal teams. The $2.5 million Gitksan/Wet'suet'en land claim action, which ended in 1990 after three years of trial, is an example. It is also a testament to the enduring attitudes of cultural superiority held by people of power within the Canadian infrastructure. Chief Justice Alan McEachern, in his Reasons for Judgement, states his belief that 'aboriginal life in the territory was, at best, nasty, brutish, and short.' He also suggests that, prior to White occupation, 'the Indians of the territory were, by historical standards, a primitive people.' Other legal actions have resulted in more balanced decisions – for example, the *Sparrow* decision regarding Aboriginal fishing rights. ¶ The communication arts are being employed to tell the First Nations viewpoint. Artists, writers, filmmakers, and performers are using modern media in addition to their traditional cultural ways. This book is part of that trend. What has historically been a non-written or orally transmitted culture has come to utilize many media. The result has been access to a much larger and more varied audience. ¶ The First Nations of British Columbia are ancient and have always had something to share. The sharing was once more equitable – until smallpox and flu epidemics resulted in great population loss. Among my people, the Kwagiutl, the population went from

10,700 people in 1835 to 1,854 people in 1929. The tribes had well-defined territories, and these were respected. Originally, there was much trade between Natives and non-Natives. The First Nations have shared much with their new neighbours. What the Native culture has to share today is not technology but a knowledge, spirituality, and approach to living with our earth that are thousands of years old. Much modern medicine has been derived from ancient Aboriginal methods. It is only after we peel away the layers of ethnocentrism and lay aside feelings of cultural superiority that we can hear what the chiefs and elders have to tell us. ¶ It is becoming apparent that technology and development are only part of the equation. Economics has become the main ethic of Western society. This system of 'scientific materialism' means that nothing matters unless it can be measured or quantified. Humane and environmental values and obligations are left out of this equation – a world-view that is short-sighted and fatally flawed. For example, when a country adds up its gross national product, it fails to make a subtraction on the other side of the ledger to account for the lost timber, forests, and such related environmental destruction as the decimation of fish-spawning habitats. These losses represent an actual reduction in 'inventory' and reduce income and job prospects for the future. This omission is especially significant with respect to deforestation, in which case, because the resource cannot reasonably be expected to regenerate, the environment suffers a permanent loss. Any business that used this kind of accounting method would not be around long. The chiefs and elders have a different world-view to share. ¶ Included in each leader's text is certain factual information: English name, date of birth, tribe or nation, present home, and parent's names. Their Native names were also recorded but were not included because of the difficulties in correctly transcribing names belonging to many distinct languages. The name and date of birth help place them in history – today or 100 years from now. These are people from living cultures, and their age and the period they were born into are significant when you consider the stories they have to tell. Their tribe is designated as indicated by the person, not by linguistic grouping, as is the anthropological norm in the portrayal of Native people. For example, what is often referred to as 'Coast Salish' refers to what today consists of over fifty tribes from Saanich, Nanaimo, Halalt, and so on. Names of parents are important in understanding 'who you are and where you come from.' Heritage and extended family are the foundation of Native peoples' world-view and identity. When an elder asks, 'Who are you?' he or she is asking, 'Who do you descend from? What are your roots?' For Native people it is a source of pride, as well as essential, to be able to recount their respective lineages up to five generations or more. This is also practical for doing research on the potlatch, chieftainship, or even in more academic areas (e.g., marriage between tribes, migration of culture). ¶ First Nations leaders consist of elders, hereditary chiefs, and elected chief councillors. The elected chief and council form of band government was initiated by the Department of Indian Affairs (DIA) in Canada, and the Bureau of Indian Affairs in the United States, in the early twentieth century. A number of tribes, or nations, have developed various forms and levels of self-government as an alternative to this system. Under the DIA, different peoples have been divided by language into tribes or bands. A tribe typically refers to people from a given village site or area, although the northern peoples use this term to refer to clan systems (e.g., eagle clan or tribe). These bands or tribes are organized into tribal councils or nations with specific historical or cultural affiliations (e.g., Kwakiutl District Council, Nuu-Chal-Nulth Tribal Council). The tribal councils exercise varying degrees of self-government and autonomy over their affairs. It is important to remember that there is this variation from area to area, and that, in some cases, certain designations are English words for Native concepts. ¶ Historically, tribal government was based on a system of hereditary chiefs. There was a head chief for a given tribe and a number of sub-chiefs. These chiefs held 'seats' which carried 'names' and were constant throughout history; only the individual holding the position changed. Such chiefs had certain responsibilities to perform (e.g., potlatching) as well as responsibilities for territory, rivers, and so on. The system was undermined through the law on the potlatch, DIA policy, and funding arrangements. It is still in place, with varying degrees of application, throughout the Northwest Coast. In some areas, hereditary chiefs are in administrative positions, and in others, they play a more 'cultural' role. ¶ The roles of elders are still very much alive, though they too have been reduced because of the residential school system. Until the 1970s, school-age children were made to attend boarding-schools, often far from home, for all their schooling. In addition to teaching reading and writing in English, the schools attempted to eliminate Native languages and values – strict punishment being the norm for speaking your language, practising your culture, or eating traditional foods. It is now being disclosed that physical and sexual abuse perpetrated by the people charged with the care of these children was rampant across Canada. This has resulted in criminal charges, jail terms, the apology and resignation of an archbishop, and formal apologies by culpable churches, but such abuse continues to be an open wound in our communities, with the people and their descendants continuing to suffer from shame and other debilitating effects. The residential schools continued for enough generations to seriously disrupt the family system. Today, the role and knowledge of elders are being preserved and respected to the best ability of the people. The roles of elders vary from area to area and from family to family. Throughout the Coast area they are recognized as a great resource. Elders often play a role in the political process as well as in the general culture. It is their inherited knowledge, as well as their perspective (derived from experience), which is valued. In the Native way, memory or history is a tribal or family responsibility and is held and passed on by the elders. ¶ In this book, the chiefs and elders share some of their knowledge about respect. Respect is the foundation for all relationships: between individuals, with future and past generations, with the Earth, with animals, with our Creator (use what name you will), and with ourselves. Respect is both simple and difficult, small and vast. To understand it and apply it to our lives is an ongoing process. This is the most valuable lesson the leaders have for us. It is not a lesson that can be explained with the simple formula, 'Respect is …' For the Kwagiutl, the potlatch is a ceremony which allows us to show our respect in a public setting. We show our respect for the chiefs, the elders, those who have passed, those who have just come, for couples who are joining their lives and families, and so much more. Our potlatch is in a period of rebirth and growth, following the end of restrictions on the potlatch in 1951. The world is growing smaller, and, increasingly, there is the need to respect and understand our neighbours. Our Earth also requires respect. Respect yourself and you will respect others, I am told. The chiefs and elders have shared much with me. In reading their words, and looking at their faces, I hope you will feel they have something to share with you.

WORDS

[OUR CHIEFS AND ELDERS]

< **CATHERINE ADAMS**
Born 1903. Gwa'sala'Nakwaxda'xw,
Gwa'sala'Nakwaxda'xw Reserve, BC
Parents: Kenneth and Lucy Henderson

photographs also on pp. 134-5

I'VE seen a lot of changes in the potlatch – they don't really follow the old way of doing things. Everything was serious, everything had to be done just so. Today they just throw things together and give it away. The way that they act in the potlatch now! One time everything had to be so quiet – nobody walking around, unless they were a part of it. No more. The manners and behaviour, that's forgotten now. It's not the same today. ¶ When the dancers were performing everything had to be so still – you couldn't let your child walk around the floor. This is the way we learned the way behaviour is – this is how strict it was in the early days. Our lives have changed! We're living like the White man now – we don't live like the Indians any more. Our whole life has changed, every tribe has changed. We used to have to wear blankets when we went to a potlatch, just a plain blanket not a button blanket, and sit very quiet. We dress too much like the White man today and act like the White man too. They're rough – Indian people had lots of manners. We had to sit very quietly, even when we were children – we couldn't get up and run around like they do now. Even the speeches now aren't like they used to be. You had to be very serious and you had to tell the truth. You couldn't say I own this and I own that, when you didn't. And they do that today – a lot of people make up things that they have to say. ¶ We used to get teachings from the elders. When I was a child at Blunden Harbour, they had a group of girls and a group of boys and a man went and lectured to the boys and a woman lectured to the girls and told us how we were to behave and how we were to act at all times. And how we were to act in the potlatch – you just couldn't go and walk out whenever you felt like it. I remember, when we were children, my mother would take a chamber pot because you couldn't just go outside to use the washroom. That's how serious a potlatch was in the early years – it was a very serious thing. A potlatch is to show respect for family and relatives. Someone dies in the family – you have a memorial potlatch to show your respect for that person. That's why I've given so many potlatches in my life, because I've had to do it to show my respect for my relatives. ¶ Some of them they just give around money inside somebody else's potlatch, and

Catherine Adams

that isn't a real potlatch. A real potlatch is when you get people together and you been saving up for some time. And you don't just give money away; you give material, dishes, and clothing – and that's a real potlatch. Most of the memorial potlatches are done that way – that's a big potlatch. Sometimes a fella will get up and say, 'I'm giving a potlatch,' and they'll pass money around, but that's not a real potlatch. They have potlatches for memorials, for passing down rights, for weddings, for naming your child. You just can't give away a name – you have to have a potlatch to name any of your family, even an adult. ¶ I went to Vancouver and I'd take a walk to pass the time. When my first husband passed away it was anything to forget about my sorrows, and I'd take a walk around. That's when I'd see the way our people were acting. People from all over, not just from here – they were from villages all over, even the United States. I used to go home and wonder if there was anything I could do to get them to live a life the way they should live a life. Because we didn't know what alcohol was until the White man came. I used to wonder, 'How can that person be that way?' I used to run into people that I had known were raised on the reserve where I'd been – and to see them living that life. That's why I started inviting them to my place to slowly talk to them about what real Indian life is – that we didn't have to follow the White man's way of living. We

had our own life, we had a beautiful life. And I used to talk about these things. So I wanted to keep them going. I felt so bad, I felt so hurt. I'd be walking down the street and there'd be a girl passed out right in the sidewalk on Hastings or on Powell St. – some girl that I'd know and I'd feel so bad. That's why I started that sewing group, to entertain them and to keep their minds on something else. I called it Gastown Workshop when I first opened it up, then I changed the name to Saint James because Saint James Church gave us a lot of help. It was sad – it was no fun. I'd be shaking hands with a girl, or I'd be hugging her and she'd be hugging me. I'd open my door when I got home and my phone would ring right in front of me. I'd answer the phone, 'You're wanted at the city morgue, so and so has died.' The very girl that I'd been loving up and shaking hands with before I'd left the workshop! That was terrible. I was down there for twenty-nine years working with the people. ¶ The life that we lived in the village – we never knew what it was, the wickedness of the world, because it was never ever seen in the village. Nobody knew what alcohol was in my early days. What we did in earlier years we were taught right from the beginning. That's how we were to treat people, to be kind to people. We were told that if anybody comes from another village we were to treat them nicely, call them up to our house and

*photograph on
p. 172*

feed them because they had travelled a distance in a canoe to reach this village that we're living in. This is what was taught to us – how we were to be kind, and how we were to share. I think this is why we never got into any kind of mess, you know. And to be kind and to share whatever you have – if the other person hasn't got it, share it. ¶ My grandmother lived to be 120, and I learnt a whole lot from her. My mother used to let me sleep with her, and she used to talk me to sleep, and I loved it. She used to tell me Indian stories. Her name was Naknagim, 'handling the daylight.' I'd tell young people today to live the way we are supposed to live, the way we used to live. To live our own Indian way – that quiet, clean life that we lived. And be kind. This is what was taught to us when we were children. An elder is to talk to the new generation and tell them how they are to live – to live the right way of living.

AGNES ALFRED
Born 1889. Namgis, Alert Bay, BC
Parents: Gwulsalas and Puglas

WHEN we were young we were not permitted to wander around. We were not permitted to be naked when we went for a walk. We were told to always wear a blanket. This was when we were single. This was before I got married. It did not matter after we were married. We were told to sit in the house wrapped in our blankets. When we went out we had to be tightly wrapped in our blankets. They had to be tucked in a certain way, called t'at t'ata. I've heard that the White man used to say, 'We are near the people who carry their blankets around.' They said we carried our blankets around because we used them as wraps. This included the men also. The nobility wore head-bands called la la xwiwe'yi. The nobility wore this silk – you know, scarves. To keep their hair out of their eyes, they would fold it and wear it as a head band. ¶ We were not permitted to show our faces in public. We were not permitted to walk around, the K'ik'i'yala [virgins]. We would be punished even if we just looked out of the house – just peeked out. There is a lullaby for Wikalalisamega. They would slap her legs if she showed her face in public. Even if she just looked out – those are the words of the lullaby. We were told that certain young men would make noises outside the houses. You know how some young men are? They would do this to attract the young virgins. Those that ran out to them were considered to be bad. The reason for all the noise was to attract the young virgins, who were not permitted to show their faces. I played outside when I got older. I was never permitted when I was young. It is difficult to make you understand now. ¶ My Indian name is Yakoyogwa. That is a bad name – I guess they gambled with me. I guess they lost me at gambling. Whoever won got me as a prize. Remember, that is the meaning of my name – I was lost in a gamble. Our people gambled with me and lost me to another tribe. I was born at Village Island. My father, Gwulsalas, is Mamaliliqala, and my mother was Namgis. She also came from the Qwiqwasut'inuxw. Her name was Puglas. Even the White man called them by these names. They didn't have English names in the early days, the Natives. I went back and forth between Alert Bay and Village Island when I was young. It has really changed, compared to my days. They used to say to us, 'Let it enter your heart even if you are not worthy.' Those are the words of a song they used to sing to us. ¶ Well, it was very bad for a woman to have a baby without a husband. 'Having an illegitimate child,' they would say. They would get pregnant without a husband. People would say, 'The Namgis women are bad because they have illegitimate children.' I heard these remarks myself. They would get pregnant. Young boys would climb into windows. There was one young boy, they found out he climbed into this young girl's bedroom. He was going to the residential school! The parents found out and started taking their children out of residential school. This was to prevent this young boy from climbing into their bedrooms again. The reason for not accepting those without a father is because the child does not grow up properly. I have heard people say this also: 'Why did he come here?' The illegitimate children, they feel they have become a burden to their tribes. That is what I also heard. ¶ There are so many things that are different today. That was the way they were in the early days – sharing things. We no longer do this. The only time we will give now is if we get paid for it. Before they would waxapa, when they willingly gave. People have to buy what they need now. In the early days they would share what they had – they did not make a profit from each other. They shared their food. Today they no longer tell the children what is right or wrong. In the early days they would tell them what is right and wrong. They used to tell me, 'If you are invited for dinner, don't go immediately after being invited. Wait for the other guests so that you all arrive at the same time. After you eat, don't leave the table before the other guests. You must wait for the other guests and leave together.' They told us all kinds of things – even the way to sit: 'Sit up properly! Sit up straight!' They told this even to the young men. 'You're always slumped over! they would say to them. This is what the elders did not like. Galxgalwit, [coiled up like snakes], they would say. D'ixD'agwit – they were the lazy ones – those that stretched their legs out. They had to follow rules, in the early days, in everything that they did. We were well taught – you had to be careful. They would lecture us: 'No, don't go out. She's probably going out to toss her hair back and forth.' Turning your head left and right was apparently very bad. Oh, they used to tell us all kinds of things when I was young. 'Even if you like what you are eating, don't eat too much,' they would say. I guess people would think you were a glutton. Oh, nothing seems to be right, I thought to myself for a short time. In the olden days we were taught everything, starting when we were young. We are all bad mannered now. Yes, indeed. I suppose it is because our hearts have become European. You know what they say about how the Europeans are. Look at what they say in this song: 'We are now Europeans. We have cigarettes sticking out of our mouths.' This is what they call becoming a European. They sang this to those who had cigarettes sticking out of their mouths. ¶ There were many rules for the pot-

latch too. The only one permitted to walk around was the one giving the feast. They would get very angry with those that would walk around at the gathering for no reason: 'He has no manners.' Everything has changed so much today. It is because of the White man that people don't follow the old ways any more. They don't visit any more. Oh, yes. They don't like each other. ¶ We were not permitted to talk back when we were scolded. We would be spanked if we talked back. Whenever someone did something wrong, their parents had to discipline them. We would just listen – we would never talk back. They would get very angry if we talked back. 'So you want a numb behind,' my mother used to say as she spanked me. This is because my behind was going to be sore. They would lecture us, and tell us not to do anything that would be considered bad mannered and not to be so outspoken. The old people gave up lecturing because of the Europeans, because of following the ways of the Europeans. It was a song that said this. They lectured us to have respect for those around us, our relatives. It does not seem we want to recognize each other today. I guess our hearts have turned European. It has really changed from the early days, it surely has. We no longer have any respect for our relatives. We don't recognize them. In the early days we respected one another – we're not like that any more. It breaks my heart, today.

We have really changed from what we were like in the early days. In the early days they really loved one another, but we don't seem to acknowledge each other in this day and age. It is not good, the way we are now. Right down to my children. They no longer know who their relatives are. That is what breaks my heart. They are supposed to love one another, like in the early days. Our children no longer even understand our language. ¶ Today's children, you should gather them together and tell them, tell them what is right. Tell them what our elders used to tell us. Tell them the correct way to do things, talk to them. 'Don't do that,' – that is what you call talking to them. 'It is bad to do that,' they would say. That is what they used to sing in the early days. They used to sing about everything. At the potlatch, they would sing the songs all day long. ¶ 'Barely made contact,' – this is what they call it when someone is born just before dying. They 'barely grasped' the person, because that person was near death. Also, 'They caught the person on time,' they'd say. I have forgotten much these days. I guess that is what happens when we grow old. 'You're so knowledgeable,' they would say to me, 'but your sister is not very knowledgeable.' She didn't pay attention. Whenever I heard a song I immediately knew it. ¶ I never, ever drank. I have always disliked drinking because I used to see my relatives fight whenever they were drunk. It was so hard on me. I would hide under the table because I was so afraid when they fought. That is why I dislike drinking. Oh, I guess I was very young when they first brought alcohol around. I disliked it right from the start. They would fight, those that were drunk. That is the reason I dislike drinking. There was this person who knew how to make wine from canned peaches. She was called Nakwaxdaxw. There was also an intoxicant which came from the beach and which people would eat. I wonder what it was? It was also really bad. No one does that any more. 'He is intoxicated,' they would say. They would die, those that ate it. ¶ When I was young, we would not stay out too long. We were not permitted to whistle at night: 'Don't do that, someone might return your whistle.' If we whistled at night, a ghost might have returned our whistle. So we would not dare to whistle at night. We were lectured about being dragged into the underworld. A child was having a tantrum and was dragged into the underworld. Everyone gave up on him and left him. When they went to sleep, they could hardly hear him. They got up to check on him, and they could hear him under the ground. They would try and dig where they were hearing him, but he would just move. He was really crying. The people in the underworld had crooked eyes and crooked faces. He was really afraid of them. A child about the same age called him – she had crooked eyes. He

p. 180

finally agreed to go with her, and it was this child that looked after him. He consented to go to the one with crooked eyes. He was really afraid of the people with crooked eyes and crooked bodies.

CHIEF ALVIN ALFRED
Born 1910. Namgis, Alert Bay, BC
Parents: Moses and Agnes Alfred

ALL my people are chiefs. I'm the hereditary chief of Alert Bay. That goes on – when I'm gone my son will take over and all the way down the line. I'm the oldest in the family so it [chieftainship] came to me, but you got to buy it. Some people carry their dad's name and never do nothing for it. To prove that you're going to take the name and follow his footsteps you potlatch. I gave three. I was the last one to give gold stuff away – gold bracelets and gold earrings. It was only $39 an ounce. Nobody can afford to do it any more. You give a potlatch to buy your name. My dad, I don't know how many potlatches he gave – it seems foolish now. When I got married, coming up on sixty-two years ago, he gave the first $10,000 cash potlatch. I didn't believe it – I couldn't see it. ¶ When you get married you Kadsikla. All the Nimpkish people went to Village Island and we had an Indian marriage. You had to buy your wife - $2,000 – and it wasn't nothing. My dad's mom put up another $500 – that's when we got her. They gave a copper, Lubithila. That's a big copper – biggest copper going around. My uncle Dan Cramner asked 'em, 'What you want to do with this copper?' They said, 'We want our copper.' I didn't know my dad gave 'em the money – that was what he was going to potlatch with. They bought that copper back for $10,000, and that's what my dad gave away! That was in 1927. The potlatch was forbidden then, but we had to do it underhand, you know. You went to jail if you gave a potlatch. It wasn't until not too long ago that we got it back – made it legal. My dad used to even give 'em at Christmas time. They couldn't touch him – he just put Christmas stamps on everything he gave away, you know. Every time one of us got married he gave one, and every time one was born he gave 'em a name. My son's got the chieftainship now I'm retired. I've fulfilled all my obligations to potlatch – I don't have to. The only time I'll give one now is when my mother goes, and that's going to be a big one because all my family will be in it. That's going to be the last one. It was her one hundredth birthday not too long ago. ¶ Everything was backwards when I was young – hard times. Not too many people educated – not even the White man in them days – seventy to eighty years ago. Indians never really know what hard times are, even if we don't have money, 'cause the fridge is right on the beach and everywhere. You don't go hungry. You can't beat the living now, but it costs you so much money. Them days you make $2,000 to $3,000 fishing, and, boy, it lasted you a year or two!

Everything was so damn cheap. Now it costs that much just living a month here! Better living nowadays. But we lost our language now, too – very few people speak it now. When I went to school they wouldn't allow us to speak it. They used to punish us for speaking it. Kids nowadays are getting educated but I don't know if it's doing 'em any good. 'Course quite a few of 'em are going on. My granddaughter is taking up law – she's going to be ready in a couple of years. Education is very important today – a must. Pretty soon there'll be no more Indians! Once they clean up on these land claims, that Indian stuff will be gone. We'll be taxed and everything. If they buy our land, then what we got? The Indians want to sell 'em part, but they want the whole damn works! Far as the Indian goes back, where was the White man? Over a hundred years ago they had nothing, so they came and bought land for fifty cents an acre. But in BC we still own – we're non-treaty Indians. We didn't come under the treaty they have in the Prairies. My grandfather, Kodi, was the first one on this island, in 1778. There wasn't one White man on this island.

p. 181

ETHEL ALFRED
Born 1910. Mamalilikala, Alert Bay, BC
Parents: Chief Harry and Mary Hanuse

I got married to Alvin over sixty-five years ago. I guess our family and our children have kept us together. That was my life – my family. That's all I ever did – I didn't work or anything until my youngest one was about nine years old. It's really changed today – there was no working mothers in the early days – maybe around fishing time, when the canneries were open, and the oldest had to look after the kids. We never ever had babysitters – just the grandmother and two younger sisters babysat for me if I ever went out. There're lots of changes today. We always used to listen to our parents, whatever they said to us we had to listen. We had respect for our parents. We were taught to respect our older sister or brother. Today, there doesn't seem to be any respect. We used to visit an awful lot in the old days, but not today. Too many things going on – meetings, conferences – so much going on now. We all went to church, now hardly anyone goes to church. That hurts my feelings. I've been going to church ever since I was a kid – I believe in that. I always taught my kids to go to Sunday school. ¶ I would advise young people today to follow what was taught to them when they were younger. I used to go to a youth guidance centre and talk to teenagers. It's really different now. My grandson, sometimes he doesn't listen to me, and I don't allow him to wander around. I never allowed my kids to wander. Kids today, they got shows – really too busy. They don't seem to settle down their whole life – it's always go, go, go. It wasn't like that in the early days – we used to sit down and listen to our grandmother tell us stories, which is not done nowadays. They seem to listen to White people's ways now. I don't know if they will be able to speak our language. They're [school] trying to teach it, but it is so hard.

p. 157

(PAST) CHIEF COUNCILLOR HARRY ASSU

Born 1905. Wewaikai, Cape Mudge, BC
Parents: Billy and Mary Assu

THIS village is not like it used to be – it used to be just like one big family. If you're cutting wood or working, everybody goes down there and helps you – everybody just helps each other. Now that's different. It doesn't matter if people are walking by, they don't even look to see you working. See, like, before we moved here we used to live in Campbell River. We moved here, my grandfather was telling me, because you can get fish in front of the village twelve months of the year. We moved here in 1888, somewhere around there. All the people here used to work for the cannery, used to drag seine right on the beach. Oh, in them days there was a lot of fish. I know down the beach, my older brother and my younger brother, we used to go down there and lower the slack when the fish were chasing the feed. They would come rolling around on the beach and we'd just club 'em. Most we got on one low tide, we got over 300. The fish would follow the beach, chasing them little herrings, and they'd go so fast they'd come rolling onto the beach, and we'd just club 'em. And you could see the fish just solid along the beach. Oh, there used to be a lot of 'em! ¶ When I first started seining, where the wharf is, we set on slack water. We got 60,000 fish on one set! Used to be a lot of ling cod. The Japanese cleaned 'em out. Used to be seventy Japanese boats cod-fishing here. To me, I think the salmon are coming back. What happened was that in 1930 it used to be that loggers could log half a mile inside a creek or river. They took that off, let the loggers clean it up: 1938, I think, fishing disappeared. I used to put in 300,000 to 400,000 for the season. 1938, I think I got 28,000 fish - just went like that! See, what happened was, when loggers logged trees off both sides of the river, it got dry. Now it's back growing. I been after the fisheries all the time. They got 1,500 feet each side of the river. Loggers can't go log there any more. So I figure the fish are going to come back. ¶ My father, in 1890, was elected to be chief. He was only twenty-five years old. See, Wamis, his uncle, was the chief, and he didn't have no son. That's why they elected him to be chief. The Indian agent came here and they had an election. That's how it used to work in them days. When my father died and the Indian agent came here and we had a meeting, they said, 'You are the chief now - it's passed on to you.' I ran this village for eighteen years. They wanted me to go back, but I said, 'No, I'm just going to retire.' It's a lot of work - how to improve the village and all that. Lawrence Lewis and I were the ones who started the housing loan here. If any young couple just get married, they can apply to get a loan for $30,000 to build a house. That's how young people get a house right away. I also got the wharf. I had to go to Victoria. This government guy says, 'Why do you want a wharf? You never had a wharf before.' I tell him, 'It'll be an improvement for our village.' So this premier, I go to see him the next day, I tell him, 'We want a wharf.' He says, 'Oh sure, you come with me.' So I went to this guy that I was arguing with, and he tells him, 'Whatever size wharf they want, you give it to 'em.' ¶ Both of my grandfathers used to teach me and my four brothers. Used to always say to us, 'Leave the liquor alone. Anyone who touches liquor – they got nothing. Well, we were pretty lucky. We were four brothers and we were all skippers. They used to tell us what the people were like in the early days. ¶ They should really control the timber today. If they're going to clear it out, we'll have nothing to breathe. Premier Bennett, we used to be good friends. He told me, 'Everything you're saying is true.' We get our oxygen from the trees. Six of my grandchildren have been to university. I kept telling them, 'You've got to have an education to get somewhere.' The preacher was telling me, 'Soon every fish boat will have to have skipper's papers.' I told a lot of young guys, 'Go to school in the wintertime. Get your skipper's ticket or your engineer's papers. You are

gonna need it some day – it's gonna come to law.' I got my skipper's ticket and my engineer's ticket. I spent two winters for my engineer's. People used to say, 'You're lucky the company likes you.' I'm not lucky, it's just because I got both tickets! ¶ My brother had a birthday for me – I was thirty years old. That morning I told my wife, 'It seems like I just woke up' – that's what I told her. 'From now on we gonna save money.' She says, 'OK, whatever you say I'll go along with it. So three years I work twelve months of the year, I made enough to buy a boat. Since that we started just going ahead. That's the main thing if you want to get ahead. ¶ When my father was chief in 1920, they had a meeting and said, 'We're going to change. We'll build modern homes, have water running into the homes, and get our own electric lights.' He used to always say, 'We're gonna try to improve the village.' He did a lot. These young people, pretty hard for them to understand – they don't work together any more. I went to one meeting with the White people and they have the same problem, the young people don't care for nothing. Well, I guess it's the way they live. I always try to tell young people to get an education, look after themselves, look after their money, don't spend it foolishly.

p. 136

GRACE AZAK

Born 1923. Nisga'a, Canyon City, BC
Parents: James and Lucy (Moore) Swanson

I was born in Nass Harbour, a fishing cannery opposite the village of Kincolith which is situated at the mouth of the Nass River. My father died when I was very young, so I did not know him. Mother worked as a cleaning lady for Dr. McDonald and Rev. Thorn to support her children until she met my stepfather, William Moore, who was a converted Christian at that time. My mother remarried. Because of my father's faith, he was heavily persecuted – he left the Anglican Church. He joined the Salvation Army which, at that time, had just been started in Prince Rupert and in Port Essington cannery in northern BC. ¶ My parents, with two boys and two girls, travelled by canoe for close to three weeks to make a new life on the upper Nass. The village of Gitwinksihlkw [Canyon City] was then a very small village, consisting of my stepfather's brothers and sisters with their spouses and children. My father started work as a preacher in the village, until changes were made. During those years, life was hard. There were times when we went hungry, times with very little money. But to me, as a child, I would not have changed my life because of the love, respect, and care that we got from our parents and the natural beauty of our country. We ate a lot of our own natural food which was in abundance. ¶ The best change for today is education. Our young generation has the best schools to attend. They are no longer sent away at an early age – not until they enter college or university. Another change is the road. Where we used to stock up for the winter because of isolation, now we can travel by car for a couple of hours to do our shopping. Our people have a lot of opportunities – similar to the outside world. But there is a sadness because our modern ways aren't all great because of drugs and liquor, sexual abuse to young children, and mental abuse. We have sidestepped our own way of life, and a lot of respect for each other has been lost. ¶ As elders, it is our place to show respect to our young people in order to gain respect. The responsibility of an elder is to keep the family together. We have to be good examples for people around us. We have to be people that our grandchildren can look up to – we have to be willing to sit them down and tell them the facts of life. An elder is afraid for the future of the children. With all the changes and the diseases – such as Aids, which is new to a lot of people, but a fast-growing disease and a killer with no real cure – with the famines, the wars in the country, killings, earthquakes, abuses of all sorts, unlimited crimes committed each day, do you wonder why an elder is afraid? ¶ But for young couples and teenagers there is a way out. And the way out is to know our Saviour, Jesus Christ. He's our only hope for today. The so-called modern, better world is too fast. But it could be our silver lining – by leaving the destructive things of the world and pursuing your education, you can have a promising career. As Aboriginals of this country, let us walk as such and keep our ways, our laws, our culture, and, above all, our language.

p. 133

GABRIEL BARTLEMAN
Born 1913. Saanich, Saanich, BC
Parents: Isaac and Martha (Irvin) Bartleman

IN the early days, the children were taken away to residential schools. At the time, I was one of the more delicate ones – not strong enough to go away from home. So my mother kept me home. I never, ever went to school. I started to work pretty young. By this time there was mixed farming here. The mixed farming was all over the south end of the Island here. Nobody ever went into cattle. But the people here used to plant grain, oats, wheat, and barley. I got involved in that when I was pretty young. I think I started off when I was about twelve years old. I was driving horses when I was about fourteen years old. Big, heavy draft horses – some of them I had to have help harnessing up because they were so tall. Once I got them on the wagon I was OK. Those days my father had to cut his own wood – he had to stack the wood, let it dry, and bring it in in the fall. We harvested the grain in fall, and I took part in the grinding of the wheat, oats, barley, and so on. So I was pretty well an all-round farm hand. ¶ When I was about fifteen years old, I worked in a cannery. Well, I saw what I call waste. They had traps out at Sooke, and I saw them pitching fish off the scows there. I was working around the cannery as a kind of handyman, I guess. I saw many times when we had too many fish – couldn't can them all, other loads of fish were coming in. They take these scows out to the gulf there and just dump them. I often think about that. I've seen so many changes. The Canadian government stopped the Native people fishing in their own fishing grounds, which are now on the Washington side. Our people had locations out there – special locations where they'd use what they call a reef net. The reef net was named by the White man – we have our own name for it: swola, 'it comes from the willow tree.' ¶ Our language is Sen chal son. I haven't really put my mind to writing it. I got a brother-in-law here, and he saw what was happening to the language. He was a fisherman before, and after he got crippled up he worked at the school here. There was a gentleman who arrived here and said he'd like to work with Native people and their language. So he [brother-in-law] said, 'If we don't record this language, and hand it over to children who want to learn this language, it is going to start fading. The important parts of that language will start to fade away.' He did it on his own, made his own style of writing the language, and it's all on the typewriter. He did very well, and they're using it at the school now. Try and give the children a little hope. There're a lot of mischievous children around here. ¶ When I was young, still a

boy yet, all the ladies around here were our grannies and were like mothers. I was away from here for awhile, and I heard that one of my relatives up here was scolding some children one day. The parents called him up and said, 'You had better lay off, or we're going to get a lawyer after you.' This is introducing something we've never even heard of before. 'Course we had heard of lawyers, but everything ran smoothly here when the old people looked after things. We wanted all our children to learn how to live with each other. We have started voting for our leader here. The Canadian government has done very well there – they know how to pull the people apart. Voting for their leaders! It doesn't work for them [White people], and it certainly doesn't work here. See, our people are not politicians. They're the poorest politicians, really. When there's an election they just want their own relative to be elected. To heck with what he can do or his capabilities for doing the job – they don't seem to matter. They don't understand. I think the sooner that we can get over voting for our leaders the better. I really think you should be represented by the oldest one in your family. The older people should represent you at a meeting. We have to go back and remember the kindness that was here. You know, [Native people used to have] these huge houses, and they had to live together, or they had to make their own way and get out and build their own house. ¶ Twenty years ago, I thought I had learnt what I had wanted to learn from the Department of Indian Affairs. I worked for them for awhile – I did odd building for them. What I could see was that there was nobody who was an engineer – yet they'd get hired on as an engineer just to have a job. So we got led around like that for a long time. It's like a serious illness. I guess we believed in that, and believed in it too long. We're just now starting, and not only here, all over, starting to look around and say, 'You know, we are capable of doing something of our own.' ¶ If some of our younger people today would only put their minds to the education that is offered to them. We have no doctors, dentists, psychiatrists. We need them people – badly. And yet, our children are not the best of students. I know that I can only talk about the peninsula [Saanich] here. Some of our children are not really wanted in these schools because of their behaviour. Their behaviour comes from home. I think that the parents should really know what parents are for. I mean that – it's a very serious thing. Our people are marrying far too young. They have to further their knowledge before they get married. When they get married they get onto welfare. I agree with social assistance – I do – when you need it. But if it is going to spoil our young people's style of life, then it's no good for us. When you look around, that's the only resource we have – we have no other re-sources. It's all being logged away, it's all being taken away. It's a real vicious cycle once you get started. ¶ The style of life that we had – if you go back many years, we had everything we needed here. The bottom fish, the salmon, and what there was to take from the open fields. That's all our people cared for before. The kids think [it was awful that] we were having to do all these things – that we needed each other. And now, there's an envelope [welfare] at the post office. They don't need me, they don't need you, they don't need their parents' advice. They know they're going to go on living without their parents' advice. All my life I worked, and I really feel good about that. ¶ I never had a day's schooling, but I had an older sister. When she came back from the boarding school, then I got the foundation of writing numbers, and mother contributed a little bit too. When I got married, my wife helped me out a whole lot. When we were raising our kids, the responsibility was there, so I worked every day I could. I'd even take a job Saturdays, doing something, even if I just got a little bit for it. And I felt good about that – I feel good today about the things I've done. I think there're so many young people today that can't say that. I often wonder, does this bother them? We always had a garden. When I was young my mother had one, and so do my wife and I. We just go downstairs and bring up a jar of peaches, tomatoes, or whatever. I think that should be encouraged in young people. My wife and I, we made everything. ¶ When we returned from living in the Cowichan Valley for thirty-one years, we built our house. We had $10,000 assistance and the rest we put in ourselves. I like to be self-sufficient – that's something we have to talk more about with our younger people. Depending on the government – one day that's going to shut down, and there's going to be a lot of people wondering what to do. It's a coming thing, because the resources are going. The timber's going, and they put a claim on the fish that we used to take out. It's not because we totally want to live off fish – it's just that we want the right to go out there and get our own. ¶ We believed there was a Maker long before the church came out here and tried to change God to another image for the Native people. Well, we always believed there was a Maker. We mustn't forget that. I would like to see more of our young people go to a church – doesn't matter what church. They've got to have more of a spiritual life. Right now they have nothing, so they have no pride. I'm not one of these people who are crazy over church, but I believe you should go to church. I think that when I die and they carry me into church feet first, there're gonna be a lot of people who say, 'Yes, he went to church.' There're a lot of people, if they were alive, they'd jump up and run away, because they've never been to church. ¶ Young people now they don't know how to get shamed. When we were young, the older people [often said to us]: 'Shame on you, don't you do that.' They taught us how to get shamed. 'Shame on you, don't you do that. One day you're gonna be ashamed of yourself,' they'd say. So that was a teaching of the people who lived here so darned long. Today, if they tell a lie they think that's part of life. ¶ You know, we have no older people here. It's a heck of a mess. We're in between looking after our own affairs and coming off depending on the Department of Indian Affairs to lead us somewhere. For many, many years we thought the DIA was here to look after the interests of the Native people. I saw twenty years ago [that there was a problem] – how can they be serving the Indian people when they are getting paid by the government? Their true feeling is that they'd just like to see the Native people disappear so they can have more control. People today hang around here waiting for a few crumbs to drop, and if somebody should get two crumbs, then they quarrel over it. That's what the DIA has wanted to have happen, and it's happening. ¶ The style of life should be changed. I don't know who is going to do that – I guess the old people, like myself, if they keep talking about what used to be here. There's the biggest headache with children today – the TV. Children come home from school, and they're lazy.

That darned thing thinks for them. That's what's wrong. You know, this child molesting, it's quite a common thing. The result of that is, when those children grow up they're mad at the world, and they become child molesters. Not all of them, but they're mad at the world. I'm afraid we have this kind of thing. After the DIA, this is our next step – to straighten that out. I really wonder [where this started]. You hear about the boarding schools. I never went to boarding school, but I was in touch with boys who did. But they didn't talk about it that way – some of them didn't want to talk about it. It has become a very serious thing. It was hidden, and now it is coming out. There was one fellow, he was molesting his own daughters. When we get to that stage you say, 'What is the cause of this? Is there any way of stopping this?' The value of the Native style of life is just not with us any more. I don't know how we'll get back to it. ¶ The elders used to teach the children a lot. I might be speaking to a nephew, talking about a direction in life. At the very end of my talk, I might say to him, 'That's what I have to offer you. If I didn't care for you I wouldn't offer you anything like that. It's my duty to offer you something, and if you want to go on and separate yourself away from our teachings, then we haven't driven you away – then you have separated yourself.' That's the kind of sharp thing that was taught to our young people, and it made those children feel at home. [Our elders would say]: 'I'm your uncle, I'm your grandfather, we care for you.' To raise a child and give them something to be proud of [they would say things like]: 'One day I will be dead and gone, and you will think about me and all the things I tried to tell you.' Those were the teachings that came from our old people. They never gave up.

p. 148

MARY CLIFTON
Born 1900. Sahtloot, Comox, BC
Parents: Billy and Mary Frank

I was born here, in Comox, in a longhouse. There was two longhouses here still – one was empty and the other had people living in it. There used to be three tribes here and one other up the river. It was all gravel roads when I was growing up. I never went to school – I don't know why. There was a school in Port Alberni and in Alert Bay. I guess I could've gone, but my parents didn't want me to. ¶ Once, I went out clam digging with my mother and brother Andy – just the three of us went to Seal Island. My father didn't go – he stayed home. We just drifted with the tide – when the tide's going out it runs out that way. We just drifted up to the island. We pulled the canoe up, and she started digging – we were picking the clams. We were pouring them in the canoe into baskets that my grandmother had made. We just drifted with the tide to come back. When we came back I found out why my dad didn't go. We got to where he had a big fire on the beach, on top of the rocks. The canoe just got there, and he pushed the fire aside and the rocks were just red hot. He took all the clams and poured the clams on top, covered them up, and steamed them. That's why he didn't

go – he was ready to go when we got back. Mother would roast them on sticks afterwards, and they would keep all winter. ¶ We used to go to Denman Island, where our summer camp was. We went there once with my brother Isaac – he was the oldest boy. There was a big log there, so they cut it in half and he made a dugout. My brother was making one and my father was making one. We must have stayed there a long time because they finished them. When they finished them, they filled them up with water and put rocks in them – red hot. He covered it and steamed it, then he put the crosspieces on it. There were three canoes when we came back. I must have been seven or eight years old. I remember it well. ¶ We never used to have cars – it was just horse and buggy. My father had two horses and a wagon. That's how we used to travel – horse, buggy, and canoe. Today there're paved roads, airplanes – there're not many steamboats going around. Used to have a steamboat come in here from Victoria and Vancouver. They used to bring feed up to Courtenay. ¶ The potlatch was different years ago – it was fading when I was young. That disease came around years ago – killed most of it, I guess: smallpox. A lot of villages lost lots of people. The flu came around right after World War One. We lost one in our village – only one.

p. 150

CHIEF CLARENCE DEMPSEY COLLINSON

Born 1928. Haida, Skidegate, BC
Parents: Dora and Adolphus Collinson

IN 1973 I became chief, [a position which was] handed down from my grandfather, Louis Collinson, who was Skidegate too. When the chieftainship was handed down we had a big dinner and the oldest person in the village gave me a name. When I assumed the name, I assumed the chieftainship. I had a big feast and gave out gifts – we give gifts at all our feasts that we have. There're five other chiefs in the village here from different tribes, villages, and clans. They all live here now. They started to dwindle down at the other villages – there was a lot of sickness at the time, smallpox and what not. So, what few Haidas were left moved here. That's why Skidegate and Massett are the only communities left. ¶ A good chief needs to treat the people right, be good to everybody equally and work with the people. I don't overstep any of our elected bodies in the village – I just say to them, 'I'm always around.' That's what grandfather wanted. I like the elected council – the ones the village elects. I don't overstep them. I believe in our councillors and chief councillor – you got to have that in the village. Some of us older people put our heads together, talk about things. We don't neces-

sarily see they do it, but we're there. As for the Department of Indian Affairs: we mostly run our own business here in the village – always have. ¶ There're a lot of issues that face us. Like, I believe in education, lots of education for our people. It's plain to see what the White man has done to the Indian. the Indian is getting more educated today and we're seeing what the hell's been done to us! By having education we can talk more and let the world know what's been done. We were shoved into a little corner on these reserves and forgotten about. Compare our reserves to the White man's cities – no water, no sewer, no education, no recreation, no nothing. Why'd they do that to us? Now they got to correct it. It's history, what they've done to the Indian people. ¶ When religion came they said, 'Worship God, don't worship the totem poles – chop them down.' The poles are our culture. Every family, every tribe has their own crests. They had their own pole in front of their homes, symbolizing what their family represents. The poles symbolize the families, not gods. Now our culture is coming back – all of it. There're a lot of people today who teach our younger generation. Our young people are trying to learn more of our culture; dancing, carving, and so on. Like the canoe, Lootas, that was paddled up to Alaska. It was made here in the village by Bill Reid and the helpers. He had a lot to do with sparking the people. Like the

Chief Clarence Dempsey Collinson

p. 140

pole that we raised here, that helped spark the younger people to see how important our culture is. ¶ Self-employment and lots of work are areas we're trying to change for our people. Like South Moresby right now – we're fighting for parts of our Island. We're trying to get our people to have more to do with that park and the White community, because it's our land, our Island. Some of the people on the Island, I call them the newcomers – they want to run the whole thing, but we want a bigger hand in anything that happens on our Island.

(PAST) CHIEF COUNCILLOR RUBY DUNSTAN

Born 1941. Nl'aka'pamux, Lytton, BC
Parents: Andrew and Sarah (Blachford) Johnny

I became chief councillor in 1983. It is an elected position – elected every two years, through the Indian Act. This system started when the Indian agents came into the community, probably in the 1950s or so. They were so busy trying to change us that everybody had to accept the ways of the non-Indian. They told us we would never be accepted in society if we didn't. That was the sad part of the changes. At first I wanted to become chief because I felt I had a lot to offer my people. But after I got into the position of chief – I guess I never realized how many issues there were to deal with in order for our people to survive. The more I got involved in it, the more I wanted to stay as chief, because I feel we have to re-educate our people into believing in themselves – into believing that they do have rights, they do have traditional territories, they have a right to the sun, to the deer, and to everything else our ancestors never gave up. As long as we keep fighting for those things, it is an educational tool for our people – to have them wake up and realize we do have rights and try and help them understand why we have been treated the way we have been. Slowly it is changing, and people are starting to stand up for themselves. People are starting to speak up, starting to believe in themselves. When all those things are happening, they start realizing, 'Hey, this is what's been missing in my life.' Then they start regaining that self-respect and self-esteem that has been whipped out of them through the residential schools and what not. ¶ I was the first woman chief for this band – ever in our history. I guess one reason I wanted to run for chief was we felt that the men had every opportunity to do something, but nothing was working out. Their vision for our people was so narrow that it wasn't doing us any good. We wanted to let everybody see that a woman could do a good job, and maybe even a better job. It was very difficult to be the first woman chief ever. I had sat on the band council for eight years, and that was no problem because there was a mixture of women and men. But when it was a woman leader – I have twelve councillors; then, ten were men and two were women. Now that the times are starting to accept these changes, that women do a good job, the council is about fifty/fifty, men and women. Nobody's surprised any more when there are other band elections around and another woman gets in. I say, 'Hurray,' the men say, 'My God!' Men really didn't appreciate having a woman chief, although no one said anything. It was more their attitude and their behaviour that really showed that they didn't

want to have a woman chief. ¶ Everything that I know has come from being on the job. I couldn't stand the public school system. I went to residential school for five years. As soon as Indian kids were allowed to go to public school, we went, my brother and sisters. It was such a cultural shock, for both the non-Indian and Indians, that it was horrible. No Indians were allowed in the public school system, and we were sent out to the residential school. And then to try to get together and learn how to be with each other, let alone learn the whole system – reading, writing, and everything else! It was such a shock for everybody – for both sides of this community. I couldn't take it – I dropped out of school in grade seven. After I had my kids (I had five kids), I went to Cariboo College and did an upgrading course there. I had to start from grade six and go to grade ten on a crash course. ¶ I remember when the Indian agent had an office here, and I did volunteer work. When I first started working in the office, I had no clue how to use a typewriter or a telephone. And now I think back on it, and I think, 'My God, whenever I talked to anybody I used to whisper, now they hear me whether they want to or not!' It didn't take too much – learning how to be assertive. The more I started to believe that my *people* had rights, the more I believed that *I* had rights – in this country, in this world, that my ancestors never gave up those rights – the more assertive I became. All those years of rotting away in residential school, and in society, because I was told that if I kept my language, if I kept my traditional ways, kept all these cultural things, that I would never be accepted into the other society – I fell for that. I did everything that they wanted us to do. I forgot my language because I got whipped so damn many times. I got whipped for eating our traditional foods in the residential school. They tried to change my religion by sending us to church every Sunday and getting us to be on our knees half of the damn day. We had to be thankful for our breakfast, thankful for our lunch, thankful for this, thankful for that, thankful for the bed, thankful for a good sleep. All that stuff – they just stuffed religion down my throat. I call that the rotten part of my life. ¶ When I was out of residential school and dropped out of public school, I started drinking and doing the things I thought were acceptable because I saw the non-Indian people doing this. They were the only ones that were allowed to drink. We weren't allowed into bars – we weren't to buy beer or anything. They used to be the only ones to be drunk, and I used to think, 'If that's the acceptable part of society, I guess that's something I have to do also to be accepted in that society.' So I started drinking, and I kept drinking, and sometimes I wonder why I am still alive. I haven't drank for over eighteen years now. I feel good about it. I just

came to the conclusion, 'Hey, what am I doing?' It was just another part of my rotten life, where they told us we had to do these things to be accepted by the rest of society. I guess that's when I started thinking, 'Who am I? What am I?' And when I finally answered those questions, that's when I started really taking a serious look at myself – my lifestyle. That's something I'm not too happy about now, but that's something that I have survived. That's my past, and now I can talk about it, where before I couldn't talk about it. That part of me has helped me to grow to be a more understanding person. ¶ It's not necessary for Indian people to be accepted by Caucasian society – that's nonsense. When people say we need to be accepted by society, that's nonsense – because we *are* society. We, the Indian people, we are society. We have been here longer then anybody else around, and yet I was foolish enough to believe that *they* were society. I guess part of that was the rotten part of my life in St George's Residential School, where they taught us, 'You can't do this, you can't do that, you must do this because if you don't, you won't be accepted in society.' It gets drilled into you – you get so programmed that you start believing in everything that people tell you. You forget who you are, you forget everything about you, your people, your tribe. Pretty soon it makes you so ashamed of who you are. ¶ I think the most important issue is Aboriginal rights and title. I think the most important thing is the preservation of our spirituality – what's left of it. Without spirituality there really isn't anything else. To me, spirituality means believing in who you are, what you are, and practising everything that you've been taught by your elders – how to fish, how to hunt, how to preserve those fish, how to pick the berries, use the berries and traditional foods. That's all part of spirituality, because if you don't have spirituality then you don't have those things. When you talk about spirituality, that also includes the environment. In our language there is no word for the environment because we have always been taught that it is part of our everyday living. Our everyday teachings from our parents, grandparents, and great-grandparents show us how to look after the foods that we depend on, and that's part of the environment, and that's also part of spirituality. Without spirituality what do you have? You are an empty shell. You're alive, but you're – almost like a vegetable. You're moving, your heart is ticking, but you're not really doing anything that is part of you. But if you have that spirituality, then you understand why you do the things you do every day. ¶ I knew that back in the 1970s people were interested in going into the Stein Valley and logging. At that point the province had a ten-year moratorium on it, which was up in 1984-5. They again started talking about going in

to log. By this time the elders were calling me and saying, 'You can't let them go in there and log, because that's our fridge, that's our pantry. If you let them go in there our people are going to die, they're not going to be able to survive – not only because of the food, but because of the spiritual things that are in the valley.' That's when we made our position public, saying we wanted no logging in the valley. The province said it was theirs and I said, 'No, it's ours.' Many times the province has said that they're going to start building roads and have gone as far as putting out construction bids for tender. We've convinced them to at least stop and think about it and take a look at it again. So the province put together this ten-member Wilderness Advisory Committee. They went out to all the communities that have concerns like the Stein Valley. They came to Lytton, and we convinced them that because of the spiritual concerns that we have in the Stein Valley that they shouldn't do anything in there. So their recommendation to the province was that there be no road-building in the Stein until there was a formal agreement with the Lytton Band. We met with Minister of Forests Dave Parker in 1988. It was just a big fight – it was a waste of time because he really didn't care. They said, 'If that's how you feel, show us there is an alternative.' So we got together as a tribe and got a consulting firm to put a study together for us on some of the uses that we could have without logging, without building roads or anything as destructive as logging. We ended up with a seven-volume report, which was handed to Premier Bill Vander Zalm in 1991. We met with Minister of Native Affairs Jack Weisgerber, and he said he had never seen the report. In our communications with Vander Zalm, he said he had seen the report and would give it to Weisgerber so he could deal with it – and he said he had never seen it. ¶ The moratorium that Fletcher Challenge has put on logging the Stein is up in a year, and I'm not sure what's going to happen. What strikes me as so funny is that when we started dealing with the provincial government, I always said it should be government to government. But they never accepted our government. Our government – as chief and council – they don't want to accept that. They don't want to see us as a government because if they accept that then we are a threat. In our fight for the Stein, Dave Parker and other people in the provincial government have always called us environmentalists – as a derogatory term. I went to an environmental conference recently, and the provincial and federal governments were calling themselves environmentalists – in such a different way. The thing we have tried to do with this Stein issue is show that we do not want confrontation, we do not want roadblocks – only as a last resort. I said I would try to do everything that I could to receive recognition for something we believe is ours. The reason we have tried to do it like this is, I saw what was happening to the Haida – I saw the elders going to jail. I saw these things happening to people who really believe they have a right, and yet they were being thrown in jail for it, and standing before a judge, and letting a judge decide whether they had a right or not. That is really upsetting – I cried when I saw that. Our people really believe they have a right, yet we are being thrown in jail.

p. 145

CHIEF ALEX FRANK
Born 1919. Clayoquot, Meares Island, BC
Parents: Francis and Effie Frank

SOME of our younger ones can't even speak the language – too much White man! They're not learning the old ways. Some of our kids understand the language, but they can't speak it. They understand the culture, they know what's going on. They get Indian names. If I put up a potlatch like my dad did, I stand them up beside me and we give them Indian names. My boys, they all know how to sing, though they can't speak our language. They tried it, but they don't say it right. ¶ I have two speakers, Dickson Sam and Stanley Sam. One of them, Stanley, speaks our own language, and Dickson translates. When we have a potlatch, a lot of the elders speak our language and Stanley Sam has to use our language, and a lot of young ones don't understand, so Dickson has to speak English. They come from my family, and I asked them to be chief's speakers. They always come when there's something to do, like a potlatch. They stand beside me at the centre there. I ask them to go ahead and talk. They know what they're talking about. All the chiefs always have somebody to speak for them – rarely speak for themselves. Same up and down the Coast.

¶ This village has an elected chief councillor too. He's my nephew, Francis Frank. They go to all these big meetings in Port Alberni and Victoria. Sometimes they have to go to Ottawa – big people, big shots! My job is to tell my councillors to go out and do this and do that. I tell them how much to say. My father was chief, and there are two chiefs higher than I am. ¶ When I was young, there used to be lots of canoes. Now, they jump into a speedboat, pull the starter, or push a button. When I was a boy we used to have to pull our canoes down and row across [to the main island]. I made two canoes myself. You got to have tools and a sharp axe. I learnt by watching my dad and my uncles, but today I can hardly swing an axe! I can't keep track of how many houses I built – I think about twelve houses. No one taught me. I built four fishing boats – the first one with my dad, the others I built with my brothers.

p. 163

HENRY GEDDES
Born 1913. Haida, Massett, BC
Parents: Charles and Emma (Johnson) Geddes

THE Haidas used to go across to Cape Muzon – that's straight across from North Island. All those places across there have Haida names. For some reason they used to have quite a village there on Prince of Wales Island, and the Russians didn't like it. So they came over and told the Haidas, 'You have no business here. Get out!' They said, 'No.' The Russians said, 'You're gonna have to move or you're gonna be sorry. When we come back next, we'll bring our army.' They discussed it among themselves, the Haidas, and thought that if they gave up they'd be driven out of their places. They said, 'Our forefathers lived here before, so we're gonna stay.' So they made more arrows, more spears, and they practised all the time. They weren't gonna back up – they were just gonna stay the way they were. ¶ So they drove themselves day in and day out. They even made a song of it – the words of the song meant 'when you get ready.' The warriors that were ahead would let their arrows go first – as their arrows were spent, they went down and the next bunch took over. It was just like a wave! They used to perform their dances with bows and arrows and spears.

So the Russians were coming in close, and finally they got to shore and the Haidas started to perform. They were dancing and singing – the women and kids were singing. So the Russians had their guns and were all ready, but as they got closer they started relaxing. They had their guns down, and they were in close range for the arrows. The Haidas let go with the arrows to confuse the Russians. The Haidas kept on shooting so they could not get established again. They kept on holding them down, until the Russians pushed over. They finally backed off, and from that day on they were never bothered again. ¶ The first making of the totem poles – a young fella had a dream. They was across on the other side of the water. When they were coming back, he slept all the way across. He had a dream that under the sea there was this huge village and there was beautiful totem poles. This was the first time he'd ever seen anything like this – so colourful. So when he got here he told the story to his elders and they said, 'Can you describe them to us?' 'Yes,' he said, 'A lot of them were different, some had eagles sitting on top, and frogs, bears, and other things.' So they got two big cedar logs and started to make totem poles. They weren't quite completed – they were building two of them at a time. Then the tide started coming in. It kept coming up to the houses, so they brought the canoe up and loaded everything onto it. They tied the totem poles together – lashed them together. Right on Telephone Hill there used to be great big cedars. An Alaskan sawmill started logging and cut them down – I feel bad about that. Parts of those trees were sticking out and everybody tied onto them. There were Massetts from all over. So they were there for hours, and, finally, somebody said, 'I don't think it will ever go down again.' Some went that way and some went this way – different ways – and a bunch stayed behind. Eventually the tide started to recede, the water started to recede, and it got down to where it is now. But there was no trees, no earth – everything got uprooted! When the tide went out, everything got swept away. There was real starvation then, nothing to eat, no water, no wood to burn. They had a tremendously high tide, but they managed to survive. There was so many people all around the whole island that some people had started to break away. ¶ The old people used to talk about the epidemics a lot. We lost a tremendous number of people! Seems like it got started more on the West Coast – maybe further down, I guess, and worked its way around. When it hit, people were working on the West Coast – it would go from village to village. When they got to the next village, people had died in their houses. They knew this epidemic was not going to let up, that they'd have to burn it. So they burnt the houses as they went along. They kept coming this

way and burnt everything on the way. So there wasn't very many left, because they knew whatever it was was catchy. The thing the elders talked about so much was the young people – the young boys, girls, teens. They'd get up in the morning and they'd have these red marks on them and they knew they weren't gonna last. This happened about mid-summer. They said the air had a stink to it. The sun was out and hot, but there was a haze, and the sun was beet red. They couldn't figure what it was, you know? They kept on travelling until they got here – there were a few left, and a few left at Yan. Most of them came here. When I was small, as I remember, I was sick, too, when the flu hit. Oh, there was dying every day – somebody dead, sometimes two. Towards the end, there wasn't enough able bodies around to bring them to the church – they'd just use any kind of box and take them right down to the graveyard. I think the survival count after the First World War was 600 – the Skidegates had 300. The smallpox, when it came through, wiped out most of them, too. That was a bad flu, that one. So that's how come the people got together at Massett. ¶ There's a lot of marriage between the Skidegates and Massetts. When this Haida Nation started up, they had me go down there – they were having meetings, talking things over. One of the Skidegate guys got up and looked directly at me. He said, 'How much of

Henry Geddes

p. 178

this Island do you Massett people claim? We want to know.' None of the Massett guys spoke, so I got up. 'The question that you have asked,' I said, 'I can't answer that question, but I can tell you a story about that.' So I talked about how the Skidegate and Massett inter-married up until lately. So if anybody asks a Haida how much of this Island he owns, he owns the whole thing. No matter what Haida, as long as you're Haida Nation. I must have gave 'em a good answer, 'cause I got a good hand for it!

CHIEF COUNCILLOR LEONARD GEORGE
Born 1946. Burrard, North Vancouver, BC
Parents: Dan and Amy George

EVERYTHING that I've worked on I've based on the idea that Native North America was governed by spirituality prior to White contact. The leadership then looked after the needs of the people; mental, spiritual, emotional. Whatever those needs are, that's what the leaders attended to. We can look back through history and say that system was working pretty good – even though it wasn't considered progress by the White man, who came later. It was quite highly developed and civilized when you think of some of the directions we try to go now, such as holistic care for people. I'm not saying it was perfect, or we had a garden of paradise – I'm saying that we did have a system. Everything was intact; the resources were intact, there was no unemployment, education was good, bodies and minds were healthy. Everything was thriving – then we had contact. My philosophy now is that we go into an area I call 'present-day spirituality,' which there is hardly none of. There isn't any because it has been oppressed out of all people. I speak from the perspective of being a Native because that's what I am. My theory is that all human beings have been oppressed away from things that are holistic and healthy, thus hurting our self-esteem. ¶ There are three great oppressions: government, religion, and Hollywood. Government because it is based on materialistic values which don't include any spiritual values and doesn't look after people. Religion because it created a fear in people. Most religions built up a fear of God rather than building up a firm relation. As if those weren't enough for people to deal with, Hollywood came along and gave us an awful image of one another. The Hollywood image of Native people is devastating: we're savage, dirty, unreliable – all those negative things. And we still carry that, people either like us and are in love with that romantic idea of being a Native or else they don't like us because they are afraid of the savage image. Basically, what the Hollywood image has done is categorize Native people into a role. When you do that you dehumanize people. I started the Chief Dan George Foun-dation with my family rather than sitting back and complaining about what Hollywood films, videos, TV networks, and media are doing with us. Why not learn a trade and get into it and produce materials from our own perspective? We feel that the more stuff that we get out there from our own perspective, the more opportunity kids that are coming up behind us have of growing up with a positive image of themselves. ¶ I try to use old philosophies as a tool. I call it learning how to become a hunter of the city, using the old philosophy of the hunter in the forest and the respect that he had, and using only what you need for that day, and taking it out, bringing it back and sharing it with as many people whose needs will be suited by it. This changed my perspective on the city. It is a wonderful resource then – go in and hunt and get things out and bring it back home. It gives it a little more meaning – at least for me. ¶ You can prepare to go out on that hunt in the same way that the oldtimers used to: clean yourself, your body, your mind, and your spirit. Then, when you cleanse yourself, in whatever traditional way you want to do that, your visions become more clear. And your goals and objectives in working for your people stay clear. I think the other part of the philosophy is that we've had a lot of problems. What we should do today is identify those problems that we've gone through in the past, so that we know for ourselves that we're not crazy and that we *did* have some things happen to us. At the same time let's make ourselves aware so we can stop using the things we've endured as excuses for failure and begin to use them for damn good reasons for succeeding. ¶ The main reason the Canadian government is so afraid [to deal with Native land claims/issues] is because they are afraid of how much they are going to have to pay and the guilt that they have. If you can illuminate the guilt, and sit them down and say: 'We don't want all the pie – we just want a portion of it. You are still going to be a healthy, vibrant country. All we want to do is help you.' A lot of White people, amazingly enough, want to inherit some sort of guilt about what has happened with Native people, as if it is their responsibility. Sure enough we have all been part of the problem, but to continue into the future having animosity for one another, or guilt, or fear – none of those things create positive communication. I think what we have to do now, to preserve what we *do* have for the future for all of our kids, is say, 'All right, that's what happened, but now we're going to deal with today. Let's reconcile and get on.' ¶ I think the spiritual values come first and everything else follows. Anytime that I start to believe that I'm in control and that I don't need those spiritual values, it doesn't work – it jams up for me. Anytime I do anything, I work with the consultation of elders and the people – and am their tool. Spiritual values are an attitude. I term it that way because quite often people talk about using old ways and returning to old values, and a lot of people get confused – they say we don't have access to a sweat, or we can't spend a winter in a longhouse. To me it's an attitude of loving and respecting and using all the tools that we naturally come into the world with. We are all born naturally highly intelligent, loving, kind, generous, caring, sharing, honest. And if we

work in our life with those things then our attitude begins to change a little bit with all the things that are around us. ¶ I had a grandmother who adopted me – she was Blood – the Red Cole family. I've had a lot of elders who have contributed to my philosophies and my direction and encouraged me. I never intended it that way – I just sort of opened myself to following traditional ways. It seems that if elders can feel that you are open to learning, they are more than generous with their teachings. It was almost like they came and gave me gifts after they helped me along my own road. The Blood reserve of my grandmother, Mrs. Cole, they've given me a pipe that I'm going to begin, this year, to learn how to carry. I avoided it for the first few years because I judged myself and didn't feel worthy of doing that because I'm from the West Coast – and I wasn't from their family. They were Prairies and I'm from across the Rockies, so I felt it should go to somebody from there, but it was their choice. Nowadays a lot of our elders are talking about the need to recognize each other as all being Native people and not base ourselves so much on our nations. We're all people and we need each other's strength. So maybe it is their way of spurring us to do that – learn each other's teachings and make each other strong. Through my grandparents I am accepted in our longhouse, and quite often at a gathering I am called up to speak, so I know our ways as well. To me, those are all honours – those are the things I regard as the biggest honours out of life. We can be aggressive and point our finger and be demanding. Quite often this is what society projects us to be. Or we can be cunning and manipulative. The idea of what it takes to be a good businessman and entrepreneur is so opposite to what it takes to be a good human being. ¶ I was interested in becoming the chief because I picked up a number of skills off-reserve, and I've worked in the development of life-skills, social, and economic development for Native people for the last thirteen years. And I wanted to bring that home – put some of that to use. We need some development here both in life-skills and economics. I was afraid that the land claim issue was gonna pass us by. Being a small reserve in the middle of a metropolis like this, we're fast getting close to being overwhelmed. So I wanted to get this stuff in motion. I spent five years with the Vancouver Indian Centre. Along with Wayne Clark, we relocated the centre to where it is now, where a lot of Indian people live. We raised the funds for that and drew up the plans and program. We managed to purchase, through the city, a 44,000 square foot building, stripped it down to ground level, and rebuilt it. We didn't realize it, but we became entrenched in that project – working six days a week, twelve hours a day. We both

had to get out of there and slow down. When I left there, I formed a foundation with my family – the Chief Dan George Memorial Foundation. The purpose of the foundation is simple to begin with, but the dream is that the more capital we get into the more we'll expand. For now the foundation is in place for the development and training of Native people in the film and video industry. It seems all of the skills I have developed are mainly towards fundraising. The projects that I had a hand in with the film department needed dollars to do them. I was the executive producer on *The Honour of All*, the story of Alkalai Lake, and *Journey to Strength*. My idea was that we change. Rather than grumbling about things, work at it and change it – become a producer. So for the first four years that the foundation has been together we have managed each year, one way or another, to have training programs in film and video and to work in the community to produce educational material.

p. 137

ADELAIDE HAFFTOR
Born 1911. Lytton, Lytton, BC
Parents: George and Mary (James) Phillips

WHEN my mom died my grandparents took me, and from there I went to school here [Lytton]. I was here for seven years, and then I went back when my grandparents needed me. They were both sick, you know. My grandpa had a stroke and my grandma had a nervous breakdown looking after him. So I had to leave school before I wanted to. I wanted to continue my education but I had to leave and that was it. I liked residential school more than most kids did. I really enjoyed living here. ¶ My aunt gave me my Indian name. It usually comes from a relative. See, Meetwa is my great grandmother's name. I had my mother's name for awhile, but I gave it to my daughter who is in Penticton. The names are inherited from your grandparents, your great grandparents, or your uncle or aunt. Whichever name is taken [depends on the size of the] family. My aunt – see, there weren't very many of us so she gave me my mom's name. After a while, I gave it to my daughter and she gave me another – my great grandmother's. Names are always more or less kept in the family. Like, my father's name was taken over by one of his brother's grandchildren,

so he's named after my father and I always call him dad when I see him. They're more or less kept in the family, names. Some people get kind of cross if somebody takes their family name. Names are usually given at a gathering. Like now, there's somebody being buried up there, and there'll be a lot of people to feed afterwards. At the end of the potlatch, as they call it, if you're gonna name your child, then you speak up. You take your child and you say so and so is gonna use the name of my father or whatever. This is the way that it used to be done, but now that the government hasn't allowed us our potlatches for a long time, we ask each other, and then we say, 'OK, you can give that name.' ¶ I have seen a lot of changes – not for the good, either, I don't think. For one thing, I was sorry to see this local school close. Ever since this closed, and the children have been going to the public schools, there's been a lot of change. They're not interested in the farms any more. They're not interested in raising anything because they've never learned how to do it. See, living here we had pigs, we had cattle, we had chickens. The boys all learnt how to take care of those. When they left this school they were able to step out into the farm and look after it. See, my two uncles ran our father's farm, with me helping. The three of us, we ran that place – we mowed hay, we did everything. But today, you take one of the local boys, take them up to the farm – they don't know what to do! They don't know nothing. The girls know nothing about the stove, the dishes, the house, nothing – because they're not taught that. When I went to school, I was a half a day in the laundry. I was in the kitchen learning how to cook, and I was in the sewing class. We spent half a day in each, and you stayed a month in each place. If you were gonna be in the sewing room, you were in the sewing room for one month – half a day sewing and half a day at school. See, that's how we learnt everything – I learnt how to knit, I learnt how to crochet. Even the boys learnt how to make bread and pies. The boys had to get up at 5:00 in the morning to milk cows, and we girls had to get up at 5:00 to cook. Nowadays they don't know that. You get a twelve- or thirteen-year-old girl and she'll say, 'I'm hungry, mom.' I didn't say that when I was thirteen years old – I cooked for my grandma, and I went and weeded the garden, and planted the garden, and all that. I always used to help my grandma – I loved my grandma. My grandma was firm, in her way, but not cruel. She didn't forbid me anything, but she'd tell me the right and wrong of it, and it was for me to judge it for myself. ¶ Respect is one thing we were taught. We had to respect the elders, no matter who. Even if you were not related you had to be respectful of them. Today you don't see that. You don't see that at all – I noticed that. And it's gonna get worse.

People are pampered too much, even by the Department of Indian Affairs. Parents don't seem to watch their children. They start right from the parents' house – no discipline. Things were different when I was young. I got one whipping that lasted me the rest of my life. I was about twelve years old, and I was saucy in school, and we fought all the time. I got home from holidays, and my mom told me, 'Go and get some corn. We're gonna have corn for dinner.' I went out and I just stripped everything off and brought it in. She started preparing it, and she says, 'Why didn't you check before you starting pulling them off the plant?' I told her, 'Well, you might as well just go and get it yourself!' Wow, I didn't even know my grandfather was behind me! I had no stockings on, and we didn't wear jeans in those days. I got a great big welt across my legs with a saskatoon switch. He said, 'Don't you ever speak to your mother like that again!' By golly, I was gone! I went and got the corn and checked every one. That was it, no more! ¶ Now I'm trying to fence my property and build a house. I want to go back home where I can do as I like – plant and whatever. I may not be able to plant very much of anything, but I'll try! I worked farming and gardening all my life. Even in Kamloops, I worked on potato, tomato, and hop farms until I retired. There used to be a lot of farming in Kamloops, but now there's not. All the orchards are gone, all the farmlands are gone - houses, all subdivided. All that beautiful land where I used to work – there's nothing but houses. I think that's why I moved from there – they look disgusting. All that beautiful soil, the best soil there is, it's all subdivided! Farmers don't get enough money for their fruit – food is coming from the States. I watched everything, and then I said, 'Well, I'm going home to see if I can raise something around there. Raise some dust!' ¶ They're talking about logging the Stein Valley. I don't agree with that. I don't even agree with a road going in there. I have property at the mouth of the Stein, maybe fifteen to twenty acres. We don't want it destroyed. I think that is the last spawning area that is still clean. Anywhere else, like down the Coast where the salmon spawn, is all clogged up with branches and trees from loggers. They promised to clean it – they didn't. It's an important spawning area, and it's very important to us anyway. I lived there for a long time because I was born there. My parents were from around that area. I remember my dad going up there to go trap, go hunt. We got our living from back up that valley. The old, old people – the old ladies they go up there, and from those cedar trees they make baskets from the roots. Relaxation is what the Stein means to us. We don't know how to say it, but it seems to me you go up there and you're troubles just fall away. That's why we want to keep it that

way. We have always valued the Stein as a place of peace for us. When you are troubled that's where you go. We go right back up in there and we don't come out for a couple of weeks, maybe three weeks. When you come out you feel at peace. That's why we value it so much. There're a lot of troubled people that have gone up there, and we'd like to keep it like that for the kids. That's the reason why I want to build a house on that property of mine there, 'cause of those kids. Someday they're gonna have nowhere to go – no jobs, no nothing. I'm thinking way ahead. I'm not thinking of myself, I'm thinking of my great grandchildren that are going to school. And when they get out, maybe they can't find a job, they can't afford the rent – they'll have a place to go. I think ahead for my kids. Some people don't seem to think that far. ¶ I don't see anything very good for the future. It's not very long from now, I think, anyway, that the world's really gonna be in a turmoil. It's heading there very fast. That's why I want to have a house over there [the Stein], so if my family have nowhere to go, they can at least have a roof. They can at least plant something to live on, have a future coming – because that's all they're gonna have. I don't really understand what's gonna happen, but it's not gonna be very nice. It's gonna be hard. They told me about the hungry thirties. I don't remember it. This is gonna be worse than the hungry thirties –

the way I see it, it's gonna be harder on everybody. They're starving now, there's no work, and this here dope that is going around is what is going to destroy the people. The young people today – I wish we had some sort of vocational school. The ones that graduate from high school here, we put them in another place where they can do things, like working on machinery and all that stuff. Maybe they'd get interested in going back to the farm, going back to nature, instead of living where they're all bunched up, like right here in Lytton. I think that would be the best thing for them. Go out into the bush – not to destroy it but to enjoy it. Try and live the way the old people did – it would do them a lot of good. Nobody does that today. They don't know what to do once they get out there. They sit down there and they say, 'I want to go back to town.' If we only had a place where we could put the children – the ones that graduate and want to learn how to run machinery, run this farm the way it used to be run. They'd learn by doing. That is what the children really need, but they haven't got it!

p. 158

MARY HAYES
Born 1915. Clayoquot, Aesousista Reserve, BC
Parents: Johnny and Mary

WE were taken away from our parents to go to school. We were so lonely it wasn't funny. I couldn't speak their language when I went to school – I didn't know a word of English. The only word I knew was candy. They taught us English. It felt as if you pulled something from that part of you! I suppose you got used to it. They constantly taught you, every day. It was very hard on us to be separated from our families, especially if we were laid up with a cold. They were very lonely days, and you felt you needed your mother and father. I was away from age nine to sixteen. My father came for me and said that's all I needed to learn anyway. They just let him take me, but in the meantime I'd lost two of my sisters who had died while I was in school. My older sister took sick – she was already going to school. I was lucky to have her for awhile. She wasn't well, so they sent her home from school – she died shortly after. I don't know why they didn't try to find out what was wrong with her. They didn't send her to a doctor or anything. My little sister died a couple of hours after her. ¶ Most children went to residential school. The people in my time have forgotten how

Mary Hayes

they have to teach their children – like our parents did with us. A lot of people aren't teaching their children, they depend too much on the schools today. We have young people today who don't know what it means to be a parent. ¶ I was lucky. Before I went to school, at the age of eight, my father had me initiated into the Klu-kwana. That was an important thing for a member of our family. I was initiated into the Klu-kwana, which was a high standard to have bestowed upon a child. Given the standards that my parents held, I had to be initiated – there was no way out. I guess I'm the only one that's been through that since the government stopped them doing it. When they outlawed the potlatch, most of us lost all our songs. My son got married and we had to throw a potlatch. I had a time trying to get all the songs together because we have to use our own songs, we can't use everybody else's. It really disrupted a lot of people and, in the end, nobody knew the songs. We had to start teaching them. We were lucky to have tapes of people who knew how to sing them. A lot of the culture, the dances, and the seating order was lost. There were certain people in the band that knew how to work a lot of regalia. They did things really good at times, eh? There was a time they had a great big thunderbird in the longhouse, its wings spread from wall to wall. It went up four times and came down and picked up a whole whale on the fourth time. This was a Klu-kwana party. ¶ An elder was someone you really relied on for guidance. They passed on all the knowledge – the remedies that were used for certain things. My father-in-law said he could have taught my grandsons to be strong. He had to have medicine for it, but he didn't want them to abuse that strength – he didn't want them to get hurt. Elders taught you how to deal with the environment because they really respected everything – even the trees. You're not supposed to watch a tree fall – you have to turn your back to allow the spirit to escape. Even trees have spirits – everything has a spirit. They passed on a lot of knowledge because that was their constant duty. Every day they taught: 'This is what you do, this is what don't do.' You had to respect what you were taught. Nowadays a lot of them don't have that respect. A lot of them compete today. But they don't do the rituals they should really be doing. The rituals were really so a child wouldn't get hurt while he's competing, whatever he's competing for, whether it's sports or hunting seals. So they were taught so they didn't get carried away with these things, 'cause they might get hurt. They had rituals for everything. When they bathed they had to learn to bathe and ask for what they wanted. When they started hunting the seals, which was just lately, after they banned the potlatch, they had to bathe in the streams. They'd sit there with their hands on their faces, so that whenever they went to their prey, whatever they were trying to spear, the animal wouldn't look. All animals feel the presence of something strange when you go near them. They don't use these rituals today – not really. A lot of them don't do anything at all. In my brother's time they used to – even my husband, when I married him. He was mad when the boys didn't do it. ¶ In the old days people were very spiritual. They really depended on their primitive weapons. They depended on asking for these things spiritually all the time, whatever they were after. They called the person who belongs to the day, Nas. Today, they have lost a lot of respect. For instance, they would never allow children to swear. There're not many swear words in the Indian language, just two to three words they said. A lot of them, even young kids, use foul language. I never knew some of those words existed, words they use. I know them now because I've heard them use them. You had to respect everything, you couldn't think of anything negatively. You weren't allowed to anyway, unless you did it behind the elders' backs. They used to teach us to think positively about everything because they didn't want us to think anything wrong – if we did that we'd start off on the wrong foot and find things weren't going to work for us. If you did think positively it would affect your life. Things would go well for us if we would think positively about everything. ¶ All the people in my time, they forgot that they had to teach their children like our parents did us. I was lucky to be with my parents for nine years at least [pre-residential school]. Most children went to residential school, so we were able to have them after. A lot of the people aren't teaching their children – they depend too much on the schools today. They think children will be taught the way they were taught in residential school. We have young people today who don't know what it's all about – what it means to be a parent, and so on and so forth. My husband was well off, we ate three meals a day and anything eaten outside of that was apples and fruit. The only time they had candy was at Christmas, and that was just for a limited time too.

p. 156

CHIEF COUNCILLOR ALFRED HUNT

Born 1929. Kwagiutl, Fort Rupert, BC
Parents: John and Alice Hunt

MY biggest memory in being chief is fighting for survival. We have a treaty, the Douglas Treaty, signed in 1950. We are negotiating with the Department of Fisheries to have our own fishing rights, and we are trying to establish our territory under that treaty. It is something that should have been done a long time ago. People are moving into our treaty area. It's a little late, but we want to stop it there. No more! We had lots of abalone out on Malcolm Island, and divers came in a few years ago and cleaned it right out. A commercial business wants to put up a fish pond up here, but I think we have stopped that. We are fighting with whoever gives the permit out in the provincial government. We are always defending our territory to keep them out until something is settled with the treaty. ¶ We have a reserve on Malcolm Island. They are logging it now. Five people are working there from the village. We need the funds. You can only get so much from the Department of Indian Affairs and from the government. Most of the time it is not enough to go around. Logging the land is going to help us out quite a bit to do the things that we want to do. I

think the funds will go into a trust fund in Ottawa. When the logging is completed, then we can sit down and see what we can do with it. It is going to be important – how we are going to manage that kind of money. This will be a big economic push for the people. We want to see the people working. You can walk around the village and see that people want to work on their yard now. It is a good thing. They are starting to want to do things to improve their way of living. ¶ A good chief needs to be willing to spend a lot of time and know what the people need. There are a lot of negotiations you have to set up with the different departments. There are a lot of meetings, land claims, and that kind of stuff. You become part of that. It's interesting. Now that I'm chief, my business experience helps out in some ways when dealing with band business. I helped the boys in the village get five fishing boats. That took a lot of my time and was quite a struggle. I wanted to get the village back into the fishing business because that is what we know about. They hadn't been fishing for a while – they lost whatever fishing licences they had. There was a chance for us to get back into it, so I talked to the fishermen in the village. It has worked out pretty good for employment. ¶ If you are elected chief of the village, always remember that you are working for the people – that you have people to answer to. Always get their support first. I want people to remember me because I did my job and I was fair to them. When I moved back to Fort Rupert I wanted to help out. Even if I wasn't chief I would want to help the people to improve. A lot of people are moving back to the village. It is not like a few years ago, when people were moving away because there were no schools here. People had to go to Victoria or Vancouver. Now there is a good road straight to Victoria. People can ride in and out. ¶ I've been a fisherman all my life. I was about nineteen when I started running a boat. In 1969 I bought my first boat, then, in 1970, I bought another one, then a couple of guys in Vancouver wanted to get a boat, so we bought another one. It just went on and on like that till we ended up with thirteen boats. A couple of years ago I sold all the boats and built one – today I have three boats. When we moved to Port Hardy we bought that corner store up there. We put a restaurant in the back. A year ago we opened up another store. So we are into that kind of business. I didn't have much education, but I did a lot of work.

p. 167

CHIEF BILL HUNT

Born 1906. Kwagiutl, Fort Rupert, BC
Parents: Johnny and Dorothy Hunt

PEOPLE used to get married in the Indian way, and my mother was one of them. They married in a church though. She said many times she was married in a church – the Indian way. Now all these tribes they get married in a church the way the White man does, but she would say she was married the Indian way. There was no divorce at that time. I hear on the TV here Christians talk about divorce. Some divorce because they have no kids. That's what the Indian does you know, that's why he moves around. If he's got no kids he goes and gets another wife – gets separated and married, you know, because he's got no kids. It's for when he dies. You know what I mean, he never dies – the son takes his place as chief. ¶ When a child is ten months old, you have a potlatch for the kid. We're different now, these days – young fellas never say what we used to do. Another thing they used to do, they used to have to get permission to attend the feast – a flour or an apple potlatch. You've got to potlatch first for your son, give him a name. Then you get permission to go in – you can't go into the potlatch until you get permission. At that time we don't get engaged like the White people. Like in India I guess, the parents look for your wife. An uncle used to tell me, 'Marry a big girl [rank], Don't matter ugly, you have to have a big chief's wife. Don't matter ugly.' I never listened to him! This stopped forty to fifty years ago, I guess. Now they get engaged like White people. My parents picked my wife. I never hardly talked to her before the marriage. We were married on Turnour Island in the Indian way. They had a potlatch – lots of people went there that time. ¶ That's where I got my Hamatsa – from my father-in-law, Bill Matilpi. I disappeared for four days before. They gave me the name Nawis. My Hamatsa again was for my uncle and my father – they gave me the name Sum-qui-das. Every time you perform a Hamatsa, you get a different name. There was a whole house there [at the potlatch]. My brother passed me up on the roof. I go to four holes in the roof [and cry] 'Hap!' into each hole, 'cause I'm sleepy up there. Four times, and then I come down through the smoke-hole. There was a rope there. Lots of them, they drop in a canvas, and a bunch of guys hold it. One guy we used to invite, funny guy you know, comical – Willy Seaweed. Well, he went to Campbell River – there's a potlatch and there was a Hamatsa. Lots of longhouses there at that time. Well, he's [the Hamatsa] going to come through the smoke-hole. His name was Quatell. Well, this fella's holding on

to the two-by-four on the roof – he's stuck – he won't let go of the roof! They couldn't get his hands off, so Willy Seaweed's got a stick and he hits him hard. So he drops down into the canvas! ¶ Lots of changes now. Before, really, really nice people, these Indians, you know. They used to help each other. Maybe you come asking for bread, you get it. Or anybody come, you say, 'Okay, come stay in my home,' another one – 'Come stay with me.' Imagine when we were potlatching, we were all going to Gilford Island or Turnour Island. I remember one time we went to Cape Mudge, lots of bighouses, you know. You stay there, everybody happy, no quarrels, lots of stories. It was happy then, not like what we're doing now. I'm sorry to say, but when we go to Alert Bay today we have to go to a café. They're good people anyway – it's just that way today. Used to be you'd stay in the homes – never no trouble when we go to potlatch. One time we went to potlatch for four months – that's the way it was done. Some guys went to Knight Inlet and got eulachon, and they came back and we stayed and potlatched. That's all we do – potlatch every night. That's why they know the songs, young fellas, you know. That's all they do – potlatch every night! Lots of them are gone now, only a few of us left. Jimmy Seaweed's gone now, maybe only four or five of us singing. Sometimes you go to the bighouse and maybe only me singing, on the mike there. ¶ When you're chief, you have a potlatch. At that time it was different, people would get lots of money right away. That time he would throw a potlatch right away. I'm going to lend out some money, maybe $1,000, $2,000, and you pay back in a year – 50 per cent. That's what the Indian did at that time. If you don't pay that for another year – 100 per cent. Lots of people, they sell the copper. The copper is like a bank – worth maybe $10,000. And they buy, and they sell it too, maybe break it. All the chiefs had a copper at that time. All the coppers had a name. One copper was named Mamalilikala – it means, 'you take all the stuff in the house.' It was worth lots of money. Lots of different names – there was lots of coppers at that time. At that time, when a chief potlatches he builds a longhouse first, you never potlatch until you finished you long house. That's why there was lots of longhouses, you know. And then you potlatch. You never potlatched until you finished your longhouse. It's different now – they potlatch any time.

p. 132

EMMA HUNT
Born 1912. Kwagiutl, Fort Rupert, BC
Parents: Dr. Billy and Edith Nelson

I grew up in those bighouses with the dirt floors. I caught the tail-end of the way our ancestors lived. Our whole family living in those bighouses. I enjoyed the life growing up the real Indian way. They used to tell us stories when we were little, teaching us how to behave, how to be honest, and to be brave. Never to disgrace the family, that was the upbringing – we had really strict rules. Never to make them ashamed of us – wrong-doings and such. There is one thing I remember – they were very strict in the old days – never to have a child before you were married. That was a real strict rule – that was a disgrace to the family. The one that I think about is that they taught us to be honest, and to be kind, and to be truthful – that was the upbringing I remember. I always tell young people, the way I was brought up was to be honest, gracious, and to respect my elders. That's very important. When I was growing up I used to never see a fight. If the kids fight I always try to make peace. Still, today, I hate to fight – unless I have to. But I'm sort of learning how to stand on my feet now, instead of always trying to be humble, like our teachings. I think you have to be that way now – you sort of have to be on the defensive side. I don't know what it is now, it's completely different. We're trying to adopt the ways of the White people now, I guess. Today we have these chiefs and councillors and things like that, instead of our chiefs of olden days. They used to have councils to see that the village was well run. Now you have to elect chiefs and all that. ¶ I practically lived more in the White world than on the reserve, and I liked it. I quickly adopted the ways of the White people and got along with them. My teachings helped me, taught me to be gracious and honest, and to be truthful. This is still important today – I try to teach my kids that. It seems there's a lot of new modern ways to raise your kids, so I try not to interfere with sons and daughter so there'll be no troubles. Not much difference though, when I see them raise their kids. I grew up in an Indian way and today I live in a modern house. And I really enjoyed the old way, but I wouldn't want to go back. I worked as a cook for seven years and as a teacher for nine years, so that's quite a difference. I didn't have any problems adjusting to the White world – I didn't have any adjustments coming back to the reserve. ¶ My husband was the hereditary chief from here. As wife of a chief you have to be gracious, you have to be noble, and you have to be a lady (which I've always tried to be) and not disgrace the family – and always cater to the chief's

ways. We always had an open house. That's the name of a chief's wife – she's always holding up her skirt so she won't trip, catering to her husband and his guests. That's what Mudzith means – chief's wife. I got adjusted to that and enjoyed that life. I always said an Indian child and a White child should be treated alike in school, so that the Indian child doesn't feel different. This is what is good for the child, in my way of thinking. ¶ Respect means a lot to me, to respect and be respected in return. I always tried to respect people. My West Coast family used to always come and visit me when I was young. They'd come and see me in Alert Bay, and my mother and father never once complained when they'd come and stay a week. My mother would just welcome them – she was full of hospitality – a real gracious Indian. She always catered to people when they came into our house. There were very few women like her. That tradition of hospitality was cut off quite early in my life, but she kept it alive. My mother always welcomed people. ¶ To tell you the truth, there was no potlatch in Alert Bay when I was young – it was cut off. I remember when it was cut off – I was eight or nine. But it was bad – they used to sneak around, and you couldn't sing or dance. I remember my mother giving a potlatch for my father. When I was fifteen he died, and she was just determined to give a potlatch. She had $300, I remember. That was lots of money in the olden days. They had tents out on the wharf, and they were going to Rivers Inlet. They had bighouses in Alert Bay then – we were living in one. So they invited all the people who were going to Rivers Inlet. The bighouse was full, but they couldn't sing. They just gave away tubs and glasses and things. She gave away her $300, but there was no Hamatsa, no nothing, no song. They just secretly gave it away. She must have been one of the last few that gave a potlatch in Alert Bay. All of her relatives helped her, and she paid it back later on. People were sneaking out with their potlatch gifts. They were going to be put in jail if they kept it up. ¶ Then when I came to Fort Rupert I saw the dancing – secretly, in the winter time. It's real rough out here – no boats or planes can come in. They'd invite the Blunden Harbour people and the Quatsinos, and we'd have a ball here. The big chiefs would come and they'd have a ball dancing and singing here. Lots of potlatches here in the wintertime – they never banned it. I always say if there wasn't a man like Mungo and others like him who knew the songs ... that's why the old songs are preserved – on account of Mungo had that brain. Him and Charlie James kept the traditions alive carving – they never stopped. I guess Charlie James was a world-famous carver after a time, when the potlatch was banned. We lived next door to him, and he was always carving. Someone would order a totem pole or something. He had a big workshed on the back of the house. The potlatch is completely different now. We have to do it fast – one day or two days. In the olden days it went on for months and months. The Hamatsa used to go get lost in the bushes – Tom's father was lost for eight weeks. It was just four days when I came. ¶ I don't care for self-government because I don't trust Indians, just as I don't trust the White man. As you watch the ones that get elected, they get rich – they help their own family, never help others. That's why I don't believe in self-government. That's what I argue about in our village – favouritism. Yet we're all related, there shouldn't be any favouritism. I always say that in the meetings, but they don't listen – they want us to listen to them. They figure they're right all the time. I don't know if people listen to elders today – they say they do. What will happen when they have self-government? I don't like self-government. I would rather have it half Indian and half White and then we could watch one another hopefully. It was alright when hereditary chiefs ran the village – they respected everybody. But now these elected ones – they want to run the village, and they don't seem to respect what the village wants.

p. 175

MARY JACKSON

Born 1906. Sechelt, Sechelt, BC
Parents: Chief (Captain) George and Theresa Finchback

SINCE I was seven years old, I have been at this reserve. My mom must have put us in an orphanage in Vancouver. There was a whole bunch of us – sisters and brothers. I think I met just two brothers and one sister of mine – nobody else. Three days it took, in a row-boat, to come from Vancouver with my foster-parents. They used to have great big dugouts years ago, you know. We'd stop about three places in the evening. When it got dark, we'd stop here and there, get up early the next morning, and be away again. ¶ They used to go out hunting and dry fish for the winter – get all the seafood they could find, have clams and everything, dry herbs up, dry smoked salmon. Used to plant the old spuds – had great big gardens. Not like now – there's nothing at all. Before, you could hardly see the reserve for all the fruit trees. Couldn't even go through, just thick. Now you don't see anything because you can't keep nothing. The younger generation – fruit just starts getting green and they're eating them. Before, you could see the plums hanging down in the garden – that's how it was years ago – but then the union store got here. The people years ago used to go

out hand-logging, you know. Women helping them, bringing down the logs, women towing the rowboat. Just a few had gas boats, years ago. That's how it was – used to make your own living all the time. ¶ This church, they went logging, and the men went all together to sell their logs. Got lumber and everything, and built the church. This side, Blessed Virgin side, well, the women paid for that, and the other side, the St. Joseph side, the men paid for that. The middle altar, well, the whole crew paid for everything. It was all done by themselves because they had no money anyway. Not like nowadays. ¶ I used to help them [foster-parents] go digging clams and things like that. I'd pick berries for them – they'd dry them during the summer. Used to pick these wild blackberries – just spill them outside and dry them in the sun. Put 'em away behind the stove, so they wouldn't get mouldy – nice and dry. When they wanted just half a cup of these wild blackberries, they'd boil it and make lots of jam from just half a cup. Salal berries, cranberries – we used to go pick those too and mix them with apples or plums, because they had lots around the reserve. Mix that up and put it on a big board, put maple leaves on it, and dry it in the sun. Turn it over again, real nice and dry, you can roll it up, just like the chewing tobacco you see in the stores. It's real nice. When we just got married, my husband's auntie gave me maybe half a sack of blackberries.

Gave it to me for a present. Salal berries, she gave me those too. That's how it used to be. Now you can't go anywhere – too many houses. ¶ We used to have other reserves. The trees are all grown over now. There's a reserve near the chuck there, where my foster-parents used to stay with my foster-father's brother. They used to go out fishing and look for anything they could catch – ducks and that. But it's so strict now – we can't even go shoot a duck at the bay, we get fined so much. You have to get a licence or permit to do anything. Not like years ago – people used to go everywhere. There used to be a swamp over here where there's a field now. My foster-father used to get up early in the morning, go over there, sneak in with a shotgun, and try to shoot a duck. He missed it all the time, and the wife used to get mad at him! ¶ My boy, the one that does the carving, he used to get this cherry bark for baskets – you can't go anywhere now. Used to pick berries and dig roots – now you can't do anything. You have to go quite a way. If you see a big cedar tree, it might be in somebody's garden and they might shoot you! You could see them when they were coming home with I don't know how many bundles of dried fish they'd saved for winter. Used to roast them by the fire and put that away too. They had lots of food – deer meat and that. It's so strict now. Can't even go get a salmon in the river now – get fined so much. ¶ My

foster-mother showed me how to do baskets. I've been doing it since I was twelve. Used to go out digging roots, used to stay at the bay there, most of the time. She had a little shack there, there were no houses anyway, just us. Used to come over this way every Saturday for mass on Sunday. Good day, we'd go out in the boat, go look for cedar roots somewhere. She'd show me how to split them. I kept up with it. I quit for a few years when my kids were all small, you know. When they went to boarding school and that, well, I could do more of my work all the time. Used to be two others doing 'em [baskets]. So there's just me doing it now. I'd phone one lady, and she'd say, 'Ah, I'm babysitting.' 'Well quit your babysitting,' I used to tell her, 'do your basketwork.' You have to go out and look for your own cedar roots, if you know how to do it. ¶ Years ago it used to be different – far different. Everything's changing now, changing all the time. It used to be nice, years ago – people out during the summer, women making the baskets – but it's all gone now. Their husbands would go up in the woods, get trees, and put the trees where they wanted to sit down in the shade and make baskets. Used to be a whole bunch before – lots of women. Used to go way up the falls, take their lunch, go up that way digging roots, stay there all day. When the husbands get home they go up and bring down their roots for them.

p. 149

MARGARET JOSEPH·AMOS

Born 1918. Clayoquot, Aesousista Reserve, BC
Parents: Tim and Lucy Manson

RESPECT was a big word for us when we were growing up. We were taught that the meaning of respect was to have your own self-respect and respect others, to love others as well as yourself. We were raised to obey our parents and listen to what they say. Teachings we had, we had to sit down at the table – that's when they talked to us, while we were sitting down at the table eating, because a child swallows and it digests into the brain. Through digestion you put it in your brain. You keep in mind what you learn when you're eating. Through digestion you put the teachings in your brain. ¶ Because a mother and father had great love for their children, for their family, they protected their family. This is why they taught us these things. All over the Coast, it's the same in every tribe. Especially with our chiefs – they had to be very strict. Whatever people got they brought some to their chief: seal meat, fish, whatever the catch was. Even shellfish, crabs, mussels, clams – they were the only things we had in the early days, so we ate what nature provided. Things have changed – very much so. Most of us don't know how to eat what we ate in our early

days. They just go to the store and buy what they need. Most people eat that now, but we used to have shellfish, all those things – the fish. We could go fishing anytime, anybody – now we can't. Got to have your permit. It's so hard nowadays compared to our growing up days. Everything was free to us, it was our own territory and we could do what we pleased. Now it seems we have to live up to the White people's way of life – adjust ourselves to the way White people live. ¶ I can't say what the future will bring for our people. Young people are more educated today then we were. They need a full education in order to live their lives and cope with the cost of living. Education is very important – we have to have it now. The young people have to have it now. With us there was just a few out of each school that were lucky enough to go further than eighth grade. We were limited so much over there in residential schools. If we weren't doing our school work right, that was it – we were finished, we didn't go any further. Some were bright enough to work hard in school, and it was good for them. ¶ I think we had more contentment in life in my early days. We were more contented with everything, and we accepted nature a lot. We noticed the beauty of nature – of wood, of the forests, of deer, of everything. A man that fells a tree, the tradition is to walk along right to the end. It was their tradition that they had to turn away from the spirit [of the tree] when it falls. And after it's down they had to walk on the tree to give them strength, like a tree has. Because it's a dangerous job to fell a tree. When my grandchildren come to me for advice now, the advice we seem to give is to get an education – because they have to think seriously of education today. Our young people don't speak Indian – they don't understand our own language now. If I try to speak to them in Indian, they don't understand. It's hard for them to pronounce our words. They lisp a lot because the only language they know is English. They really lost it. A few understand it, but they don't speak it, you know. ¶ I think to the non-Indian money is so important. That moneymaking business they have in mind all the time. They're not taught like we were taught in the early Indian days. Then everyone shared what they had. Even if a man had felled a tree, they'd share the wood with somebody else – that's how it was in the early days. Now you got to buy everything. A man would be selling wood, like the logging industry. It's altogether different from the life we had in the early days. I guess that all I can see is that money is so important to non-Indians because that's their main thing in life – to provide for their families. Like everybody else – like us now. Because we live on our pension we can't work, we're too old to work, and we haven't got high school education like young people have now. Looks like that's going to be the way it is, the way it's going. The tribal council has these meetings urging people to take on their cultural traditions. Still, it's hard for people to really understand the value of our culture, the traditions and ritual rites which they had in the old days.

p. 154

COUNCILLOR CLARENCE JULES

(Ex-Chief, Kamloops Indian Band)
Born 1926. Kamloops, Kamloops, BC
Parents: Joe and Agnes (Duncan) Jules

I went to the Kamloops Indian Residential School. The only part that I remember that I didn't like was getting strapped for speaking my language. When I went there my parents spoke Indian only. When you get strapped for speaking your language it really does something to you – it takes it out of you pretty near. You don't speak your language any more. Like, I can understand it perfectly, but I don't even try to speak it. Whether or not that part comes naturally after the strapping I don't know. Not too many here speak the language – a few, though. That's the only beef I really had with the school – it was probably the best system we had around at that time. Maybe we could have had it better, but we didn't. ¶ I feel education is all-important today. Let's face it, here in Kamloops we all want our culture back, but we got to make a living in today's world. The Kamloops band, they're mostly real estate people, eh? They deal with leasing – big leasing, you know. We make about a million bucks a year out of leasing. We learnt through the school of hard knocks. We thought we knew what leasing was, but we've come along with it. I'd say we really understand it a heck

of a lot better than when we started in 1962. ¶ I was chief from 1961 to 1971 – something like that. I was asked by some of the guys. I was on council before that. I'm the only chief to be elected by acclamation three times. It's quite an honour for me really. I stayed on because it seems like if you get to pushing something, you want to follow it up. And leasing has always been my own thing anyway. I lease property of my own, outside of the band. I do good at it too. It makes a pretty good living for me, but I do other things too. ¶ I'd say today that employment and making a living is the big thing. I think the booze and drugs go along with that. I think a young fella thinks all he can do is booze. When they really come out of it they go religious – Indian religious, I mean. They take up their Indian heritage and they want to do something for the band. That's the only thing that takes 'em away from the booze and the drugs. I don't know why that is, but anybody I've seen who quit drinking and quit smoking that stuff goes that way. When I say getting our culture back, I mean speaking our language, for instance, and going to sweats. I know some who still carry it on. Hunting and fishing – let's face it, it's getting to be a historical thing. To hunt and make a living by it – you can't do it. Speaking our language and remembering who we are as Indian people is our culture today. Know who you are as a person, from within. We've been to quite a few meetings and heard of kids being adopted out. All of a sudden they find out they're Indian kids, and they start running away, going back to the reserve. They really want to know who they are, where they come from. ¶ My dad was a real good farmer – a heck of a lot better than I am! With what they had then and what they could do with it, and what I have now and what I can do with it, he must have been good! It was mostly farming here. When I was a kid everybody had a dairy cow, a few head of horses, a few head of cows. Today it's not like that, eh? I would say, long ago, in the line of vegetable gardening, you couldn't beat it around here. It was terrific. Today most people just go to work, eh? Leave at four, come home at six, no more working out in the garden. Me and my wife used to put in a big garden. We got a few acres, eh? We put in an acre of corn, about the same of potatoes, tomatoes, about 360 plants at that time. One night all our corn was gone – stolen. About an acre of it gone, just the day it was ready. All the potato plants were turning brown. We went out there to find out what was going on, and about every other one of the potatoes were gone. So we just gave it up – we weren't gonna do that for anybody. ¶ I think self-government is inevitable. If the Indian people are ever going to get away from Indian Affairs dominance, it's the only way to go. I think the Sechelt went a

little too far – they're right out under the provincial government. But they haven't gone completely out of the Indian Act yet. The way I see it is, it's OK for you, maybe, but what about the other guys coming behind? How are they going to take it? How are they going to push it along? All it takes is another chief, an ambitious one, and you can be right out of the Indian Act. You've got to look at least twenty years ahead of you. Just envision what you think will happen in that time. As a leader of your people, you've got to do that. How are you going to do best with what you have today? The band here is under Sections 53 and 60 [Indian Act], and some of the bands are talking about band enhanced powers, changing the Indian Act. But when you look at the people under Section 53 and 60, they should try to improve that area, only that area, stay within that area, and not go beyond that. I think the Indian Act is really for the grassroots people. It's there for the protection of the land. Let's face it, we just haven't got the sophisticated way that the White man handles land yet. And until the Indians reach that level, I would say we have to be under the Indian Act. We have to keep our Indian reserves, or it will be gone in no time with nothing to show for it.

p. 144

CHIEF BERT MACK

Born 1924. Tuquot, Ucluelet Reserve, BC
Parents: Cecil and Jesse Mack

I notice that people today talk about traditions, our culture, and how they want to learn more about it. I think they should look into the other society also because of the changing of each era. Even today we would benefit if we knew both societies [White and Native]. I'd say around 1930, when everything was going downhill, they didn't bother with the other culture either – they didn't belong any more. This is what my father was always saying, 'You got to get to know both ways to get along and to understand people.' I don't know how many of the chiefs have got that idea, to try and understand both worlds. I've always understood our culture – we never lost it, my father never lost it. I never lost the language and I believe that, with my knowledge of our Native language, I have a little more understanding than the average West Coast person. ¶ I'm going by what our culture is and what our traditions are. I have a speaker who does the speaking for me, and I have the head of our wolf clan, which a lot of the tribes have lost, too. They haven't kept up to the rules and regulations of the Klu-kwana. There are very few of the tribes that are still into following the traditions.

The Ahouseats are one of them that I know who have a head of the wolf clan. I've got my own, and I picked both these people through their family background – I didn't just pick them at random. They come from the knowledge my father gave me. ¶ The way I see Klu-kwana is – it is our constitution. The way of life, the law, the power of life – all the way from the law to the dancing culture. A lot to do with handling medicines, a lot to do with fishing, which we lived on. The whale hunters used to use it a lot in their ceremonies before they went out. That was usually handled by the Klu-kwana, that's part of it – social, political, economics, everything. It was so strong that the head of the wolf clan had the power to put people to death. It wasn't the chief that had that power, unless it was due to circumstances. It was the strongest of all the powers. That's why I term it as the constitution, because everything hinged on that – that's where everything came out. ¶ It was usually the chief that put this Klu-kwana feast on. He could invite anyone he wanted to initiate into the clan. It went down to the sub-chiefs, too – they could call a Klu-kwana feast. It wasn't just anyone, you just didn't go to the chief and say, 'I want to join – here's my money.' You had to be asked. When I put on a feast I co-hosted with my tyee, Lawrence Jack, and I had the right to invite people who I wanted. I invited two from Neah Bay – they haven't had a Klu-kwana there for years. So these two people have the right to wear the black face paint. They can do the dances without anyone saying they're not Klukwana. The initiation used to take a month, my mother and grandmother used to say. When that was finished it was followed up a year later. Nowadays it's just a day – I don't think I've seen one that lasted more than four days and then come back a year later. ¶ The biggest issue today is the government that is supposed to be in control of our lives. The most pressing issue I know is the liquor the White man brought in. I think the worst physical disease we have is alcoholism. I'll say one thing – we're trying to stop it. In most parts of the country its treatment is new – we don't know how effective it is. I know in our country here on the West Coast, they have quite a few facilities where they send people in to be cured of this disease. But what happens to them when they come out – that's where we're failing again. We haven't got anything for them to do when they come out. But I think they're looking into it now. Too many people are concerned about that end or it – when they came out they were ignored, same as when they were drinking. ¶ I think education is one of our big moves towards understanding our culture and traditions, plus what I call the other society. I think education has a lot to do with that. Seems to me that the more education our people are getting, the more they want to understand our way of life – the previous lifestyle. In 1930, when everything went down the drain, it was the government really starting to interfere with the life of the Indians. They were shovelling kids into these institutions, where they weren't supposed to speak their own language, and were trying to get rid of their traditions and culture. When it did start back again in the mid-1950s, it was a real battle even to get started on it. I was fortunate to be one of them that never lost thirty years there. My brothers, who weren't getting that training that I got, were in the same position as the young people of that time. Most of them can still speak our language, but the young ones are in that grey area where they understand it but don't speak it. ¶ I'd have to go back to education again – once young people learn how to use that knowledge it spreads to other parts of their lives, and they can go back to the traditions of our people. I believe, too, that if a young person has an ambition to go through the education system, they don't usually have that much time to spend in the bar. They have more to do, they have more to think about. One of our spokesmen has been saying this to young people; that the traditions and culture of the people were lost years ago, and we have a new culture today – that culture is Friday and Saturday night in the bar. That's what people look forward to.

p. 122

CHIEF JOE MATHIAS
Born 1943. Squamish, North Vancouver, BC
Parents: William and Elizabeth (Jacob) Mathias

I believe that we as First Peoples of this country have inherent rights from our first occupation. Our rights are not granted to us from the Queen, the Royal Proclamation of 1763, nor the Indian Act – not even the Canadian Constitution. I believe that rights – Aboriginal rights and freedoms – they all belong to us and we have to protect and preserve them by standing up for them. Because if we don't do it, we know that White bureaucrats, politicians, and governments were not set up to look after our rights. ¶ The rights are there, they exist, but they must be recognized, affirmed, and respected. Aboriginal rights to the fishery resource, for example, are inherent rights. They belong to us – they are not granted to us, as White governments would have you believe, by a piece of legislation. What we are saying, what we have been saying for decades, is that these are our rights, rights that derive from our ancestors, the first occupants of this land. They continue because we're still here. Our rights are not here to be bartered away and extinguished. Our rights are here to be recognized and respected. We want the freedom to exercise those rights for all time. ¶ Aboriginal rights are already entrenched in the Canadian Constitution under Section 35.1. What we need is some sort of guaranteed process, a constitutional process, to elaborate what these rights are – not so much a definition of, as an elaboration of, Aboriginal rights, and the process to implement them. What we're talking about is not a shopping list, or a wish list, but an elaboration of what our rights are. ¶ Our position is that the Supreme Court of Canada, under the new Constitution, has a broad interpretive mandate. They have to give meaning and breathe life into a living document called the Canadian Constitution ¶ We are distinct, we are different, we were here first, and we possess inherent Aboriginal rights that belong to us. And what we want to do is to establish a relationship between Indian people and White society, and that relationship is now framed in the Constitution.

p. 146

CHIEF RODERICK ROBINSON

Born 1931. Nisga'a, New Aiyansh, BC
Parents: George and Pauline (Adams) Robinson

I went to school in Alert Bay when I was eight years old. My mother had typhoid fever, and I stayed there for nine years. There was no assistance in them days – you had to work in the canneries, doing jobs like unloading salmon. Quite a number of us went to high school and paid our own way. I would have gone to university, but I didn't have the funds and my parents couldn't afford it. Some say it's going to be the salvation of the Indian people when we get into these institutions of higher learning – we will get into fields of endeavour such as teaching. In those days, the ambition of just about every Indian of my age was to be a teacher. I think, to them, that was about the only objective within their grasp. You didn't have to go to university in them days – you went to what they call a normal school. Doctors, to us in them days, were like gods – they had the power of healing. And lawyers, with their fancy words and mouths – little did we know that we also had those gifts, that we were just as capable of doing it. But we had to have the opportunity. ¶ Before, the Nisga'a were self-reliant – there was no welfare, no unemployment insurance. Somebody received it one year, and it went all over the village in the 1970s. People were saying, 'Hey, this guy worked in the cannery, and now he's getting cheques!' Geez, it astounded our people! He went from house to house with the first UIC cheque. You've got to remember we're isolated – there was no road for quite some time. ¶ I have been the executive director with the Nisga'a Tribal Council for about five years now. I've been chief councillor three times now, and I've been on the council for the past thirty years. Before the Indian Act, the authority of the Aboriginal people was with the Council of Chiefs. All the head chiefs were in the council – but now, anyone can get elected to the position of chief councillor. That's the creation of the Department of Indian Affairs. But our own system is in existence. We go by the matrilineal system – this has been going on since time immemorial. The name that I use, that's been given to me by virtue of my ability to communicate, speak my own language, know my own history, and know my own songs – as well as being conversant in English, as limited as my ability is. I can express myself much better in Nisga'a. By virtue of that, and by virtue of my rank, I assumed the name. So when I go on to the happy hunting grounds, the next in line will take the name. So the name lives on, but the people, who, since time immemorial, have been wearing this name, have come and gone. ¶ We have a four-clan system. I'm the head chief of the eagle clan. You have the frog or raven clan, and you have the killer whale, and then you have the wolf. So those are four clans. One clan was almost wiped out when the lava erupted here and 2,000 people perished. So there used to be five – the Gisk'ansnaat, they call it. They're starting to build up again. It is strictly against our tribal laws to marry within clans. As hereditary chiefs, like myself, one of our responsibilities is to be stewards of the laws of the Nisga'a. And one of those laws is that it is forbidden to marry within your own clan. I cannot marry another eagle – I married a wolf. She's one of the remaining clans that almost got wiped out. When they realized they could not support our tribal system, they sort of amalgamated within the wolf clan – they're close to the wolves. If I do that, marry within my own clan, then that's going to weaken the clan system – it's going to destroy our ancient law. ¶ It's not what we, as Nisga'a chiefs, want, it's what is required of us. From the time that we are born we come under the law of the Nisga'a. We are given a name, even when we are little babies. We begin to be groomed for what lies ahead of us. We begin to be educated in our own ways, and one of those is that we have to make ourselves available to our people – to serve our people. We don't run for office. To this day, even though the younger people are orientated to the White man's elective system of campaigning, mak-

ing promises, and this and that, it's still not used. ¶ You don't campaign. The people will look for the person that they want – someone that's courageous and has the ability. So we really don't have a choice. But every Nisga'a out there is ready and poised to serve in any capacity. There's no such thing as, 'Oh, I decline' – that's strictly against our laws. In this day and age, you have to avail yourself if you're nominated or elected – you just have to give the nod. It's not a choice each Nisga'a has, to run for these offices – it's by virtue of our laws that we make ourselves available to our people. They themselves will tell us, 'Let a young man take over now. You've done enough – you've made your mark.' So we just step aside. It's just like going on a trail – you can only take the lead for so long and then you get tired. ¶ Foremost on our agenda is the resolution of the land question, because we have no treaties. We come from a tradition of defending our territory. Where it is recorded, it says that the Nisga'a were foremost in this struggle. We don't know if this is the truth or not. Maybe the other groups were doing the same thing. I believe you have to give credit to the whole movement, here in Canada, of Natives trying to assert their rights. We were just one of many groups who were concerned about the encroachment of the White man. ¶ Years ago we were told that the lawmakers were across the sea, over in England. So our people, with the assistance of the missionaries, drafted what is called the Nisga'a Petition, which was sent over to England, supposedly to be dealt with. A law firm was hired over there, and it was not dealt with. Even on this side, you put in all the papers, and they're not dealt with until five or ten years later – that's how slow the judicial system of the White man is. If they want it to be swift, then they make it swift. If they want to delay it, then they delay it. ¶ Today we have signed an agreement-in-principle with the federal government on the framework for negotiations. At the moment, the framework is empty – but we have described what we are going to be negotiating. We're going to be negotiating compensation and land; resources such as fisheries, forestry, and minerals; and self-government – the power that we had before the White man came. We want that to be recognized so that we are a self-governing nation. What we want are the proper resources to operate self-government. We have also agreed to the rules concerning how we are going to negotiate. Right now, the compensation – we have not said how much we want. It will be up to negotiations to determine compensation – how much land we are going to get, what will happen about the fisheries – the whole comprehensive package. We have been very careful in our wording with regard to the province. We know that the province will one day come aboard – attitudes change, the resistance

of people changes. From a better understanding of one another attitudes *do* change over time – governments *do* change. So we have left it open for the province to step in. At this point in time, they're saying, 'We don't recognize Aboriginal title.' That's their position – that's their bargaining position. That position is no different than the federal government's – they agree with each other that, 'if Aboriginal title did exist, it was extinguished, prior to confederation, through certain land legislation.' They have a policy concerning how to deal with the Aboriginal land question. As a result of the work which we were a part of, we were able to get some recognition entrenched in the constitution, Sections 31, 35(1), and 35(3). So we made some progress in the constitution. ¶ Aboriginal title has been described in many forms. It is mentioned in the policy of the federal government, but it has no foundation. Aboriginal title means, as said by the late James Gosnell, 'We own the land, lock, stock, and barrel.' That's what Aboriginal title means. Based on our spiritual belief we are part of the land, we belong to the land, we are God's creation. Therefore, our identity is tied to the land – the land's where we live. We have certain spiritual beliefs about that land. So Aboriginal title is ourselves – we are tied to the land. Aboriginal title is White man's terminology as well. We had to search for a word that would be understood when we first went to court, so we used that word. But sovereignty is another word. We were sovereign nations when the White man found us. So we own the land and all the resources: the air, the rivers, the streams – that is Aboriginal title. We are tied to the land. ¶ Our spiritual belief differs from the White man's spiritual belief, which says, 'God created man, the earth, and every living thing. Man was to have dominion over all of the other creatures.' In other words, man was superior – he was there to exploit. And now they're over-exploiting. But us, we are different. Our spiritual belief is that we were created as part of the land – so our identity, our names, and our songs are all tied to the land. That's Aboriginal title. So we cannot be separated from our land – we have to remain part of the land. That's the basis of our Aboriginal title. ¶ We have a philosophy which allows us to manage the resources better than the White man. Because of our spiritual belief, we cannot abuse nature. We cannot take more than we need – we have to be mindful of the future. This is our basic philosophy – there's tomorrow. So when we take salmon we only take what we need and we protect the salmon. We want to see an integrated management regime that's based on our approach. All of the trees, all of the streams, are one. You cannot be extracting one resource, such as minerals, at the expense of the land and other resources. Each resource has a role to play in our survival. ¶ We have the proper philosophy to manage, and we've been trying to influence the government to see it from our point of view because we see destruction coming ahead. For example, look at the valley here. What future is in store for our children, for my grandchildren, because of the clear-cutting in the Nass Valley here? We would have allowed them to log here, if they'd have asked us. But we would have said, 'As you cut one tree down, make sure you plant another one,' so within so many years there would be a continual harvest. But now the multinationals come in – because of greed, they allowed them to come in here without proper negotiation with us. That's what we're trying to do today – get a treaty that will legitimize the presence of the Crown on our land. Right now, according to us, they're squatters – they're on it illegally. They've stolen it, in plain language. We're trying to achieve certainty, which will describe how we are going to share the land and co-exist. If you take a look at history, the European immigrant has totally ignored the rights of the Aboriginal nations. They've stepped on us, arbitrarily taking away our land without signing a treaty with us. They put us on reserves – we didn't want the reserves. They said they would 'protect us,' under the constitution, Section 91(24), but 'that land you are living on will not be yours, it will still belong to us.' The land is still held in trust by the

Crown. The government has been trying to rule us for the past 100 years. I believe it was their greed to get at the resources that motivated them. ¶ We had laws, similar to the law of the land. The Canadian constitution dictates power – it is the supreme law. The same with us here. We had a supreme law – the Ayuukhl Nisga'a we call it. It dictated how we were going to live, how we were going to resolve our problems, and so forth. So we had self-government. The government says, 'No, you people were no better than animals.' They did not know about our institutions of government. This is something we'll have to examine as we begin to unravel the various attempts of the European immigrants to solve what they call 'the Indian problem.' That's *their* Indian problem – not ours. If you begin to unravel it, you will begin to see that was their position, that 'the Indians are no better than animals – they are inferior, therefore we can step on them, take away their land.' Back East, there were some tribes that were shot on sight – they had bounties on them. This was the mentality of the day. I often wonder, in the thirty years that I've been up front, dealing with the various levels of government, if that thinking of the eighteenth and nineteenth centuries still prevails today.

p. 179

GRAND CHIEF
JAMES SCOTCHMAN
Born 1918. Lillooet, Lillooet, BC
Parents: John and Nancy Scotchman

I used to go with my father to meetings – that's where my education started. Then I went to school when I was eleven. I went to school for a few years, but I was taken out early to look after the old lady because the old man passed on. There was a principal at the residential school that wanted to keep me going. He told me I had something in my head that he wanted to develop to help my people. But I was never able to go back. I learnt a lot since, though. I used to go to university extension courses. That's how I learnt to look after the orchard out back. I went to a chiefs and councillors leadership course at UBC. ¶ I was chief for twenty years [1946-66]. When I was voted out, the White community of Lillooet picked me up and I was vice president of the Chamber of Commerce for two terms, and I became its president for two terms. That's as far as the constitution went.

p. 165

CHIEF ADAM SHEWISH

Born 1920. Sheshaht, Port Alberni, BC
Parents: Jacob and Eva Shewish

I'LL tell you what happened to me just prior to my father's death, because this is how a chief thinks. One of my uncles and I were going to put up a Christmas party. We got all ready, then my late father got sick, so we called it off. New Year's Eve, I didn't think he was going to make it that night. He called me – he says, 'You going to put up a party for the tribe?' I said, 'Yes.' 'Better put it up tonight,' he said. 'No, no, we'll wait until you get well,' I said. For the second time he says, 'Better put it on tonight.' He says 'Son, put that party on tonight. Remember, you don't count – it's the people that count.' He said, 'You got to serve your people – the people come first.' We put up a party New Year's Eve, everybody came. Believe me, my heart wasn't in it. I had to show in front of people that I was enjoying it. And all that time I knew my father was going to die that night. Shortly after we went to bed, the phone rang – I heard my uncle get up. Soon as he started crying I knew what had happened. My father's last word to me was, 'Remember, you don't count – it's the people that count. They come first.' So you can see how I was brought up. I learnt the ways of a chief from my father and late uncle. When I was a kid I was taught to go without – the people come first. I was brought up to always give more than my share. ¶ I had responsibilities bestowed on my shoulders without anybody putting them there. When my mother died and my auntie took over – without being told, first thing in the morning – I would go to the well and get some water. Then I'd cut a few blocks of wood, split and pile it inside, then go out hunting for either duck or deer. I had to do it because I figured they needed my help. I was raised with a lot of respect for my elders. Today there's not as much of that as I'd like to see, though my own family, they're very good that way. ¶ One time I was visiting my cousin, and I was called up to the hall. We were in town ten to fifteen minutes at the most when we were called. We got there, the usher opened the door, mentioned my name, and everybody got up. I was escorted to my rightful place, sitting with the chiefs. Nobody sat down until I did. Then, soon as I sat down, they chanted a prayer song and they told the people, 'Our chief is home.' They presented me with a rattle, presented my late wife with something else, and we sat down. To me, that's something that I'll always cherish – because I was treated like royalty 'cause they knew who I was. ¶ My father died in 1951, and I have been chief ever since. We tried the electoral system under pressure from the Department of Indian

p. 139

Affairs. It didn't work. Three times the DIA tried to make it compulsory. Each time there was an election we would lose a year while the new chief got acquainted. I don't know how many times it went like that. The tribe wanted to go back to the hereditary system. ¶ I never tell the people what to do – I try to show them that what I'm doing is right. We go get clams, and when we get back my two grandsons know exactly who they're going to give them to. It was my late aunt who told me, 'There's someone up there looking after us. You share with the people, whatever you want to get it will be easier for you to get it next time. It will come back to you.' I found that to be true. It's easy when you start sharing with somebody. It's so simple to say thank you for the day – no harm in that. First thing in the morning you ask for safety in that day. A few minutes of your time, yet it means a lot to you. ¶ I think I'm very just to everybody. I never take sides or anything, I just let them thrash it out themselves and come to their own conclusions. If I get an idea, I let the councillors or one of the people in my tribe come up with it. Let him think it's his own idea – instead of me telling them guys what to do.

LUCY SMITH

Born 1931. Gwa'sala'Nakwaxda'xw,
Gwa'sala'Nakwaxda'xw Reserve, BC
Parents: James and Ida (Seaweed) Henderson

WE couldn't go to school in a regular school because we were half-breeds, my brother, sisters, and I. We did finally go to Indian school, where we weren't allowed to use our own language or anything. If we got caught we'd get punished. Years later my dad found out about this school, and I went to school for three years. I went from grade one to grade eight in that three years. By then I was twelve. There was no way you could go to high school – they just wouldn't let you in the 1940s. I guess Indian kids were allowed, but we were half-breeds. We were neither White nor Indian – we were nothing. We weren't accepted by the Indian people either. ¶ My dad used to have us at Bones Bay in the summer, and I used to notice that the Native children didn't really like us, and the White children didn't like us either. It was hard on us, but when I grew up I used to hear some of my other friends – they didn't want people to know they were Indians. I used to wonder why – why don't they want people to know? It's something to be proud of. *We* always were – we had grandparents at home who spoke our language, and that's when I got interested in language. I realized we

Lucy Smith

were losing it – nobody wanted to speak our language any more. That's when I took that off-campus language course. I was forty-six. I taught and went to night school after that. I taught for ten years altogether. ¶ An elder is a person that knows the history and knows the background of the other people that live in the village; knows names, how to fix different traditional food, how to pick it and prepare it; and, if a young person comes along asking questions, that elder should be able to answer them. To me that's an elder. You're not an 'elder' just sitting in a rocking chair getting old – you should have some answers! Elders aren't valued as much today. People are living in fast lanes now – they don't have time to stop and smell the roses any more. They're too busy with their own lives – they don't have time for the old people. I'm only fifty-seven and I've noticed this in my life already. It won't continue though. I think there's going to be a turn-around if enough young people realize what is happening now. They want their language back, they want to learn the traditional things in Indian life – the food, the berries. They want to know about that – they don't want that to be lost. ¶ Something important to pass on to young people is the abiltiy to be self-sufficient, to get food from the water, to respect other people, and to keep the environment clean. I teach my grandchildren that, and I teach them to be bilingual. We're still a real close family – we still have big suppers once a month, even in this little trailer. It's just standing-room only. I think that's the kind of thing you have to do to keep the family together. ¶ At one time they used to have a bighouse, and a grandmother and grandfather was put there, and they were the babysitters. Now it's changed – a young person gets married and moves away so they don't have the bighouses any more or the grandparent tucked away to babysit. I think that's a lot of it right there. It had to change – the world's going forward all the time so it had to change. I think there will be good things in the future for Indian people if the young people would just stop, look, and listen. That's all they have to do. We have to start looking after things – our water, our seeds, our crab beds. ¶ I was about six years old when a potlatch was held at Village Island. It lasted about four days. All the women had to wear blankets, and as they were going through the door they had swansdown put on their heads. When that was put on my head, this old man from over there said: 'Now you will never be able to go home. You belong to our tribe.' I remember screaming, thinking I could never leave! ¶ I'm happy right here – I wouldn't change a thing. Even if I won that lottery I wouldn't change anything. We are happy living simply. The only thing that I might do is travel to Scotland and see where that part of my family came from. Get in touch with those roots.

p. 153

(PAST) CHIEF ED SPARROW

Born 1898. Musqueam, Vancouver, BC
Parents: John and Matilda Sparrow

THINGS are working out for the better for our people, but it will take a long time. We have to change – the only way now is to get into the way of the White man, I guess. Otherwise you'll never get nowhere. You got to get your education and everything else and go out and compete. You'll never do nothing on a reserve. The only thing we have is lease-income of our land. If you don't go off the reserve you never earn a decent living. Self-government will work if it's planned properly. First of all, the government has to give us something better than they're offering us now. We have to hold the money from taxation of our land. It's our land! We have to get some kind of income from our resources to guarantee us that we will succeed in self-governing. If we self-govern now, how will we tax the people when they're living on welfare? The majority of the people are living on welfare, eh? The reason why – I use the word discrimination! You don't last at a job very long unless you're a very good man. Like, I hardly lost a job when I was in the logging camps because I *worked* there – showed the guys I could work along side of them, eh? The foreman can understand that

– he wants things done. Then he favours you when he sees you doing your work properly. I worked on the boom for six to seven years – head boom man all the time. I think if a man works hard he'll do all right. That's common labour though, otherwise you have to educate yourself pretty well. ¶ I think we got to change our ways. We have to educate ourselves and forget about depending on bloody welfare and government. Education is very important to our people. What if the White people didn't have an education – where would they be now? Sword-fighting and one thing and another! It's very important to educate our children. They can go out for an education, sure, but they can live here and modernize our place – help the people to do better for themselves. ¶ I don't know about young people; sometimes I wonder. They don't talk to you hardly. We were taught to respect our elders long ago. Talk to them, help them. Now they just look at me when I pass by – say hello sometimes. I don't know half the people around here. They don't mingle with one another hardly. People used to have a gay old time! Used to get invited together to talk to one another in the field or playground or something, and they'd talk, talk, talk – tell one another old stories and one thing and another. Now you don't even visit one another hardly – all reserves the same way. ¶ I don't think things are going to change if we don't change our lifestyle. We got to change our entire life, I think. We got to go off the same way the White people are doing – we got to go out there and compete. We got to educate ourselves and go out and compete. If you don't do that you'll be looking around for work all the time. Very few people working on the reserve now, you know. Some work in the city; twenty, thirty, forty, fifty maybe working outside. Most of the ladies are working off now. Seem to be educating themselves better than the young people are doing. I guess they're looking ahead to the future better than we men are. ¶ Seems to me there's too much good time now. Too much good time, not enough work. That's not good for anybody. How you going to raise a family? Most people here have big families. How you going to raise a family on welfare? How are we going to educate them? I don't mix much with the old ways. Once in a while I go to please the people that like to see me there at Indian dances and gatherings. Once in a while, sure, go enjoy yourself – once in a while. But not every night or every week. ¶ Yeah, well, things have changed a lot since the old chief died, eh? Things began to – well, us younger guys took over then, eh? Used to be people were having short lives and what not. There were outhouses, and we didn't have running water. People were drinking well water. All the surface water is contaminated around here. That's the first thing I did, was get running water – that was in the 1940s. After we got running water people got better. We got up quite a few dollars and we started building better homes for our people. We started out in a village down there by the water, but I thought to myself that it's too damp down there, so I started a village over here. We built about fifteen to twenty homes for awhile. My son took over then. ¶ I became chief in 1954. I was the first elected chief. My son John was the second. People asked me to try to lead the people, eh? I thought, 'I have no time for that, I'm a fisherman – I can't lay around.' Most of the time I was fishing or in the logging camp. So I settled down here for awhile. I would have to quit fishing and come home for the day to try to get things going. I had to quit being chief – it just interfered with my own life too much. I was chief for four years. Usually we'll only have a chief for two years, eh? Always somebody you know. Hardly enough time for anybody to make any improvements – just get things going and you're gone again. The next guy comes along and he's got a different idea. I don't think that works very good myself. I think it should be at least four years. I guess an honest guy, with some sense in his head, makes a good chief. Only problem is, with the elected system, they think it's an honour to elect someone as councillor or chief, but sometimes they're picking the worst guy on the reserve! They're not doing the man any good by that system, I think.

p. 168

LILY SPECK

Born 1904. Tlowitsis-Mumtagila, Alert Bay, BC
Parents: Jim and Elizabeth Harry

I was born in a longhouse on Tourner Island – both my parents are from there. Everybody lived in longhouses in those days. My parents arranged my marriage to Henry Speck. We got married in the Indian way – we Kad-zi-klaed. All the tribes came to our wedding potlatch, and my father gave away gifts and money. We did Indian dancing all night when I got married. They used to have a plank, and the man used to have to run up a plank to try and get the woman. That's how they did it in the olden days. It was a test, if he gets her. I was nineteen then, and my parents did not want me to get married right away. I was the only daughter, and my mother wanted me at home. I didn't go to school – that's why I don't speak English. ¶ They don't follow the old ways in the potlatch today. When they make a speech nowadays, the dancing, and what they take from the families – they go ahead and use it even if it isn't right. The potlatch is different – everybody wants to do it their own way. People don't care what they use any more. They take something from another family – they don't ask and they go and use it. A lot of us old people know when we see it. And they say things in the speeches that they shouldn't say. Young people today don't understand me, even if I try to talk to them. They don't speak their own language – only English.

p. 173

HAZEL STEVENS
Born 1900. Haida, Skidegate, BC
Parents: John and Fanny Cross

I'M a Raven [clan] – an eagle is opposite. They're not supposed to marry each other [within same clan] – I'm not supposed to marry another Raven. An eagle can't marry another eagle – it has to be opposite. They all got different crests, designs they use on their dance blankets. ¶ When I was fourteen I started working in the cannery and I just loved it, just loved it. I'd never seen anybody hand-filling cans. I used to get six cents a tray, twenty-four cans to a tray. But I managed to buy my clothes with it, whatever I made – winter clothes, summer clothes.

p. 142

CHIEF CHARLIE (JAMES) SWANSON
Born 1921. Nisga'a, Greenville, BC
Parents: James and Lucy Swanson

I'M a hereditary chief of the frog clan. There're also wolf, killer whale, eagle, and raven. In the raven clan, there are different crests – there are frog (that's ours) and flying frog. In others, the crest is robin or robin's egg – they're different. See, in the wolf clan they have the bear, howling wolf, circling wolf, and there're a lot of other different crests. In my family, it is the starfish and the frog. That's why the head chief has two crests on the blanket. See, I'm the head chief of our tribe. ¶ I was born in Greenville. I was raised up in Christianity. I don't know too much about places of the world. I worked in the cannery when I was fourteen to fifteen years old. There was lots of drinking at the cannery. I didn't care about it. My mother said, 'You watch what you do! You don't drink – don't you start doing that. Somebody might throw you overboard, off the wharf.' I listened to her, and I never go near that stuff. ¶ Before the road it was really quiet in the villages. There was all kinds of activities going on. Second week of the month there was band practices, choir practices, church army service on Wednesday, full service on Sunday afternoon and evening. As soon as the road and the bridge were built everything was different. Every Sunday people went away – going to bingo or down to Terrace looking for something to drink. We used to have a beautiful church service – now it's empty every Sunday. Just six, seven, eight, fifteen people is the largest congregation I've had. Ever since the bridge has been built it has taken the people away from the community. But I don't mind that. ¶ When I was ordained priest I made a vow, right in church, to the bishop, not to be discouraged – not to mind what's going to happen. The service is yours and you're the boss of this beautiful church, and if you fail you're gonna hurt so many people. Let the people do as they please, but you, you are different – you're a priest. Doesn't matter if there's one or two in church, keep on going. That is what I'm doin' now. ¶ This is what happened in those days. When I was nine years old, there was no teacher in Canyon City. We were taught just A,B,C, like that. After everybody joined up with the Salvation Army, the divisional commander, he put a teacher there – an elderly lady. We managed to learn a little. But the first week of March, my parents took us to Fishery Bay, and we spent about a month and a half there. In May, they took us down to the canneries again. Therefore, our education was very poor – not like modern education. There're all kinds of warnings now – if you miss school your allowance

will be cut off. There was no allowance, no unemployment insurance in them days – nothing. What you make fishing, that's the little money you have all year. I was going to go to residential school in Chilliwack, but my parents held us back. Now I can study all the time – it helps me quite a bit. My only qualification now is translation, Bible translation; hymns, prayers. I translate the Bible into Nisga'a. I'm the only Native Indian that received the bishop's diploma. I went to school in Arizona, Vancouver, and Toronto. The bishop sent me all over because I have a poor formal education. I didn't realize I was gaining quite a bit – I didn't feel I was learning anything until the big test. I went through seven different workshops until that night when I wrote that final test – 200 questions and I managed to get 179. That's how I got that bishop's diploma – and I'm the only Native Indian [who has one]. ¶ I've been a Christian all my life, although I failed after I got married and went into drinking. My mother always said, 'I always brought you up to be a Christian – I never want you to carry on. I'll soon die. Who's gonna take my place? It's you – you better make up your mind about quitting. Besides, you have such a big name, a Chieftain name, and you don't want to disgrace that name. You want to be a respected person.' So I thought it over, and after she died I quit everything. I quit drinking in 1980. I used a self-cleansing feast. I called all the people, apologized to the people. I told them, 'I've had enough of this miserable life.' You can't go back to that kind of life again after you use that feast. When you finally decide to step out of that pleasure world and change your lifestyle – I don't think there're too many people who can use that kind of feast. If you go back to where you left off, they're gonna call you the dirtiest names – 'cause you never lived up to your own words. When you call the people, they're the witnesses. I apologized to all the people, from the oldest to the smallest. This is on Tuesday, and on Wednesday I got converted – asked the Lord to forgive me for my sins. Those two together, it's a very hard thing to live up to – it takes a man to do it. There're only two or three who can do that feast. When I finally made up my mind, I was ashamed of myself – I had offended so many people. This is in the fall, and in the spring the bishop came up and asked me if I could join this ministry: 'After one year, you pull through, you gonna be ordained deacon if you make it.' I was really happy – I'd been wanting to be a leader in the church. That time I made it through and I was ordained in 1981. I've been faithful in my work. In 1984 I was ordained priest. ¶ Preaching works both ways. I like it more in the Nisga'a language. This is what the bishop said: 'Don't try to make a White man out of yourself, you're Nisga'a. Don't try to talk English in the gatherings.' That's

why I use Nisga'a in Canyon City. The old people really enjoy the Nisga'a sermon – they want to hear more of that. I'm talking about the real old people now. ¶ Years ago, this is what happened when Christi-anity swarmed this great Nass River. The priest that was working against totem poles and the potlatch was J.B. McCullough, up by Old Aiyansh. He was working behind the backs of the people, you know. He didn't consult with the people before he arranged for the totem poles to be taken out of the Nass River area. He did that behind the peoples' back – the whole Nass River. That's where all the cutting down of the totem poles began. They cut them down, took them down the river – that's why you don't see any totem poles. There used to be a lot of poles across the river. That's where the mass killing took place, due to the navy boat that came up that river and started supplying liquor to the Indians. At that time there was a mass killing, because the Nisga'a had too much strong drink. They used to drink home-brew, according to the stories, until the navy boat came up and did a lot of damage to the people – brought liquor up by the case. From then on, that's when the potlatch was banned, along with totem poles, and dance blankets. Our culture was condemned at that time. But later, a lot of people turned Christian. They reaffirmed themselves and they reaffirmed our culture. ¶ There're still some people who speak against our culture. There're still some coastline people, down this way – they don't want to use it. They've no use for blankets and dancing or whatever. Nothing wrong – that's the way our forefathers dressed, I tried to explain. The Hindus have their own vestments and culture – so do the Chinese and Japanese. I said to them, 'Why do you look down on our own way of life? That's the way they dressed.' People make all kinds of excuses. I used to use my Indian blanket in church, you know, the old church. The people said, 'That's the reason why we don't go to church.' I tell two of my deacons, 'Well let's take them off, we'll see what happens.' We never use them any more, but still they never come. Another excuse! ¶ After my brother died in New Aiyansh, that's when I took it [chieftainship] over. When I die, my brother Chester Moore is going to take it over. He's going to be my successor. It goes by age. It goes to the brother or the nephew – not a son. The son is different. See, my wife is wolf clan. The chieftain is the peacemaker. The chieftain is not supposed to say anything to hurt other people. A chieftain is an overseer – more or less an instigator, with the younger people behind him. His job is to tell them, 'Don't do this, don't do that. If this job is good, go ahead, do your best.' A chieftain is not supposed to go and sit in the bar and holler, 'I'm a chief.' Nobody will recognize him or respect him there be-cause he doesn't belong in the beer parlour. His life is not supposed to be seen to have bad habits, like drinking with a lot of people. His appearance will build him up, if he has a good public appearance. To be a head chieftain, or any other chieftain, he's supposed to be a peacemaker – to encourage the others. They're not all good – I'm telling you, some of them are bad. ¶ A chieftain is not supposed to speak badly over little things – he is supposed to just sit there and wait, wait, wait. It takes about two or three hours to get over it, and you're a happy person. If something is wrong with my son or daughter, they're having problems with somebody, and I start squawking on the phone or go out and see these people and ball them out, well, then I'm not a chieftain. I have to sit there and wait, wait, wait, and things will be different. I always said, 'Things will be different.' I'm a praying man. I have to be like Christ. Christ didn't do that, go around hurting people. So being a chieftain is a lot of responsibility. You have to tell the younger people in the family, 'Don't do this, don't do that.' When they do that, the blame doesn't go on them, it goes on the big chief – 'Why don't you tell your nephews or nieces …' They would talk to me personally, and say, 'Why don't you train your nephews or nieces?' You have to hold yourself down and wait patiently – like a storm. A storm passes through some time after – that's the way I take it.

p. 155

CHIEF SAUL TERRY

President of the UBCIC
Born 1942. Bridge River, Vancouver, BC
Parents: Nelson and Ella Terry

I didn't even want to become a chief. I guess it was the condition that I found our people in when I went back to the community in 1970. It was a situation where I found that there was no electricity in the houses, no central heating, no children in our homes. They were being shipped far away to residential schools or other situations like that. I guess it was being woken up to that reality that prompted me to continue on. I had promised some of the chiefs there [home], after they'd been after me for a couple of years, needing help. They thought I was educated and that I'd be able to help because of that education. So I reluctantly agreed that I'd give three years, and after that I'd come back to my stone sculptures and what not. When I was teaching art I'd tell people, 'I'm doing fine, thank you very much, so don't bother me with superfluous things.' But when I got back and saw the actual situation, then I started to really investigate the history of the Indian people in this province and country – and especially of our people. That was a rude awakening to me – that prompted me to say, 'OK, I'm prepared to serve for awhile.' ¶ I was elected chief in 1973, then we started to work getting electricity. They built a dam on our river, and they diverted the whole river through a mountain for electricity for Vancouver. That was back in 1959, and we had no electricity twenty years later! We got electricity in 1974 and all the other amenities that should have been there already. We brought our children back from Kamloops and other places. You know the trauma of parents who never really cared for children once they became school-aged, and they said, 'What do we do, how do we help them?' They were panic-stricken, in a sense, because the children never were home except in the summertime – a month or two and away again. That's the kind of situation we find ourselves in. We, as children, were not only being separated from our parents, but separated from one another – boys on one side and girls on the other side. And the junior boys were separated from the older boys, so you were further isolated from your brothers and sisters. I guess what happened was we all grew up as strangers to one another. People wonder what's the problem nowadays, why we can't relate to one another and stuff like that. That's the cause of part of it – the separation. ¶ Those were the kind of realities that started to creep back into my life. So I guess I was starting to get educated again. Because of this outside education system I was assimilated, I guess you could say. Then this reintroduction into the community and receiving education, that was not given earlier, as to who Indian people were, who I was, what role I played in this whole life – that was a whole different education process in itself. ¶ The question of the land is the most important question facing Native people today. Last November the general assembly of the Union of BC Indian Chiefs directed me to pursue the treaty-making process. Most of my energy is directed in that way – in settling the land question with the government of Canada. That's where the solution is for a lot of the difficulties our people encounter today, whether it's political, economic, cultural, social, or spiritual, because our people have been targeted for repression and oppressive legislation and policy for so many years. They have attacked us in their various ways and by various means. They outlawed the potlatch in 1884 – that prohibition was in place until 1951. Same in 1927, banning the lawful assembly of our people to fight for our rights and raise money to fight the land question or to hire a lawyer. Because the government of Canada was afraid of us, and still is. That's why they're concentrating on having us accept something less than fair for the land. The government is afraid, especially here in BC, because we still have title to our lands – so they have no legitimacy. I think you could say, technically and legally, that the BC government is an illegitimate government because we have not sur-rendered title to our lands – so we still have supreme title to our lands in BC. In national/international law that is the reality. ¶ One of the main reasons they outlawed us in 1927 went like this: 'Look, if we proceeded on that premise [aboriginal title] there'd be chaos.' And so it is for the sake of not wanting chaos that they continue to maintain their policy, as illegal as it is. Is that any way to pursue something, to maintain the people in an unjust situation? I don't think it will be chaos from our point of view, it will be just a matter of realigning, and a sharing of a power and a sharing of resources from our lands. That's what they're more afraid of – the sharing of the power and resources from our lands. They want it all for themselves – they just want to be able to maintain the status-quo. They want to be able to say, 'We're the boss here.' They want us to just go away, but we're not going to go away. I think Indian people are very astute in terms of being able to manage our affairs. And I think they're afraid maybe we'll be too successful, so they have to enact policies and legislation to keep us in our place, as it were. ¶ I think a lot more people have begun to appreciate and understand the importance of the environment for the continued existence of human beings as well as birds, animals, and fishes of the sea. So that's why we now have a tremendous concern for the environment. You hear talk today about the environment –

I don't know how serious they are about it, some of them. The land of ours, the air, and the sea are very important. Although they're using a lot of rhetoric in that area now, the governments have to begin to respect the land. So, I think this is where they've learned from us. We have been speaking out for so long and have finally been proven correct. It gives one a good feeling. I think, if one sits down and thinks about these things, modern scientific knowledge coupled with the hereditary or traditional knowledge of the people is a powerful instrument for resolving a lot of the difficulties encountered now. I think the difference between the Native and non-Native attitude is appreciation of the environment versus the past lack of appreciation by the exploiters. If we don't respect our lands, then we are sentencing future generations to a destroyed environment, in which, perhaps, it would be much more difficult to survive. If we don't look after the waters, the land, the air, and the environment in which much of our natural foods grow, we'll be sentencing our future generations to a situation of want, if not starvation. I think it's a matter of survival to be able to protect our territories from destruction so that future generations can exist. If we incorporate these kind of things into a treaty with the governments of this country, then we'd really be assuring our survival beyond the twenty-first century rather than giving in to the termination or extinguishment agreement that the government now wants. ¶ Self-government means you want to be the boss over what happens to the people on a day to day basis and what happens to the people in the future. We have to be able to make decisions to protect our people, the lands, the water, the air, and so on. That's what the government's role is, to protect and ensure that there's a continued existence past our time. I think that's a very important point that a lot of people don't appreciate. They want it now – immediate pacification or benefits with no concern for the future. That's what self-government is – establishing something that we can safeguard for the future. It's your traditional way that you carry on your day to day, year to year business from generation to generation. You pass it on – that's the respect and recognition of the reality of how people look after themselves. It could take different forms in different areas, depending on how the people see themselves operating and protecting themselves and their land. That's the challenge I see in treaty-making – to be able to accommodate all of those differences, to be able to address the reality of each group, their strength and diversity, and still have the common principles to protect the rights of these people.

p. 159

AGNES THORNE
Born 1906. Halalt, Duncan, BC
Parents: Ed and Madelaine (Dick) Norris

I was born on Valdes Island. That's where my grandfather came from. It's really different now. When I was young, everybody was really happy – always together. Everything you do is in helping each other. Now you don't help – you have to pay. My dad used to give the old people deer meat, fish, ducks. Indian way, you help the old people. Long time ago, the old people used to help each other. I think it's all right to help people – that's the way it was from a long time ago. People used to depend on each other. One would go hunting, get deer meat, and divide it for everybody. Sea lion – Indians used to eat sea lion – now we go to the store to buy meat. White people stopped the Indian from getting the deer, now it's the clams – we can't go get clams free. You have to get a licence – you got no licence, they put you in jail. It's really bad now. Everything used to be lots. You know that dog salmon? Used to be lots around here. My mother-in-law was the last one that dried dog salmon. Spring salmon coming up – you can salt fish, save it for wintertime. Now you can't do it. You have to go to the store all the time – buy something. One time I was home, a young guy said, 'Three jars of clams.' I said, 'How much?' 'I just give it to you,' he says. I was just used to everybody selling something. He was giving it to me and I thought he was selling it! Used to be different – give away anything. I don't know what year it started to change – long time ago. My mother-in-law used to give everything away – dried salmon, potatoes. My father-in-law used to plant potatoes all the time. Some people used to own a bighouse – used to go give them dried salmon, potatoes. It's different now, everything is different now. Some say it's no good now. I like the way it was before – everybody was friendly with everybody. Now it's different. These young people! ¶ The White people are stopping us from getting deer meat, stopping us from clam-digging. Everything used to be free. Crabs – you can't get crabs. Some guy getting crabs in Pelican Bay, and he's White. Guess he's got traps or something. Indians can't get it. It's hard for us to – sometimes I wish for my own food, the Indian food – clams, ling cod, rock cod, everything. We used to be happy on Valdes – never used to buy anything, just the flour, potatoes, sugar, and tea. If you're hungry, you'd go fishing and get fish. You want a change, you just go to the beach and get some clams – all kinds of clams. White man has taken away these things – I don't know why. They're blaming the Indian for finishing the fish, but I don't think it's like that. Long time ago, it was Indian food, the fish – long time before the White man got here. Cowichan Bay had lots of clams. You can't get them now – too dirty. ¶ I didn't go to school. My dad didn't let us go to school. Only school used to be on Kuper Island – only school for Indian kids. My dad was over there, and he didn't like the way they treated the kids over there. He says, 'I'm not gonna put any of you guys in there. Either you'll run away or something will happen because it's on the other island. Can't see you there, and it's one year before your stay is up.' You can't speak your own language or you get punished. That's why the Indian, he really lost his language. These young people can't speak their own language. That's what I tell the kids, 'I didn't go to school, and I don't know how to write. Can't talk English good. You kids, the school bus going around, and you still miss school.' I think it's important for these kids to go to school – they'll learn. It's not like before. You can't get a good job if you're not smart [edu-cated] and can't read. My grandson's wife went to school for four years – she's teaching now. Everybody goes to school now. ¶ They still got the Indian dancing – can't stop the Indians from that. Only the potlatch – they stopped that now. Used to be, summertime, it was outside. Now the White people really stopped that one – I guess because that potlatch was different – give everything away to

the people. That's the way it is for the Indian. If you do something, you give something back. I don't know why he [Whites] stopped it like that – he tried to stop the dancing, but he can't. The next one is Friday down at Cowichan – lots of people, I guess. Bighouse – we call 'em longhouse – it's full now. My younger sister, she's an Indian dancer, and so is one of my brothers. Me, I'm not an Indian dancer. ¶ People come to me all the time. They want to know their family tree and all that the Indian knows. This is what elders do, if you re-member the names. If I've heard the Indian name, I know it. Some, I never heard 'em called their Indian name – just know the English name. One couple sat here last week, asking me the Indian name. I don't know the Indian name of that lady. I guess they're gonna name themselves this weekend – big dance. You have to tell the people to get named. I didn't like to go to the bighouse to name my grandchildren – I just went to the hall. I named all my grandchildren – I named thirteen that time. People today respect the elders – just some of the young people are no good, never respect the old people. Me, my grandfather taught us when we were small, 'Even if you don't know the old people you help them. Don't make fun of the old people – you're gonna be old too.' We used to be helping the old people. We used to respect the old people – give them food. My mom used to cook something, then we go around giving to old people. The old people thanking us, thanking us. You help – you do that for the old people. Some people respect the old people. I like my friends – I don't like to be against anybody. I try my best to be nice to everybody. Now I'm old – not long to live, and I don't want to be against anybody. Some people are really against each other. My grandfather taught us – every day he talked to us. My mom and dad never taught us anything – just my grandfather. 'If I don't love you, I don't tell you anything. But I love you, that's why I tell you something. I want to be proud of you when you grow up.' That's what my grandfather used to say. I was thinking about that. That's right what he said – my grandpa. Some people get really mad when they are correcting their kids. My grandfather used tell my mother, 'Don't get mad at them, just talk to them. Say you're correcting them, and if you're shouting at them, they will never listen – they're just scared, they will never get what you're saying.' I think that's right too. My grandfather used to just talk to us – all of us. He would tell us, 'My sister, sit down, I'm going to talk to you. The one that is listening to me is gonna know what I'm saying – the one that don't listen to me is gonna have to ask what is going on.' My sister asked me something, and I told her, 'You were there too, listening to my grandpa.' She told me, 'I forget now.' Parents never teach like they did in the old days. Now, they try to ask the elders to teach the kids. Lots of kids coming to me to ask something. ¶ Not too many young people speak our language. The residential school, I guess. They couldn't speak our language – you get punished all the time. Kids now speaking English since they're small, but us, we used to be speaking the Indian language – my grandparents, my dad, and my mom – always speaking to each other in the Indian language. They're trying to teach the people the Indian language in school now. I don't know what's going to happen. Only my nephews on Valdes Island, they're all speaking the Indian language – and their grandfather's a White guy! Some people are starting to learn their language. They want to get it back, their own language. I think young people are taking an interest in the culture. The old people know traditional knowledge, but not the young people. The young people don't know anything. ¶ I don't know if things will be getting better – it's totally different now. The young people are getting wild, like White kids. My grandfather taught us, 'If you see something lying on the ground, you don't pick it up.' My grandson got home one time (I raised my grandson – my oldest grandson) and he says, 'I got a knife, mom! I found it!' I tell him, 'Bring it back where you got it.' He says, 'I found it.' I said, 'What you gonna do if you lose something and

p. 164

maybe you go back looking for it? The owner of that knife may be looking for it now, and you got it. You put it back.' He run away, and he put it back. Lots of these young Indian guys are taking dope now, and alcohol. They just drink, and their kids just stay home. I never drank all my life, and I never use anything. I don't know why the people drink. One time one lady said here, 'Next time I come we'll have a party. I'm gonna bring liquor.' I said, 'No, thank you, I don't drink.' She said this to me: 'Poor you.' I thought to myself, 'Poor yourself!'

SARAH TUTUBE
Born 1910. Tuquot, Port Albion, BC
Parents: Joe and Cecelia (Joe) Atzic

I was taught by my mother, grandmother, and grandaunts. They'd come and teach me how to raise up my children. I'm forever thankful for that – the two of them never got tired of telling me over and over again. There was one old guy, this great grandfather, who used to come in with a cane in his hand, walking in, very old, and he taught me how to raise up my children – what to do and what not to do with them to raise them up to be good men and hard-working, not lazy. So I'm grateful for that old man and another old lady – grand-aunt. She used to tell me about my relations. We used to have to know our relationship [genealogy]. We had to respect our relationship up to our fourth cousin. It was a no-no for the first cousin, a no-no for the second, a no-no for the third, and the fourth was just excusable when you couldn't pull them apart any more: 'Well it's alright.' They're not teaching them any more like I was taught by my mother, that's the problem. I used to teach mine. The old people used to tell me to pass things on to the next generation when I grew up. My mother used to say, 'When they're just big enough to sit up and watch you, don't you ever do something that's wrong because your child will do the same as you're doing.' That's the way she taught me. Today they won't listen any more, 'That's for yesterday,' they say. ¶ What I see in the future for the people is not very good, the way things go nowadays. We don't know what this generation is doing now. They want to go back to Indian ways but they don't do it. They want to be a White person at the same time, but they don't go far enough. I believe Indian kids need to go to some kind of university, get some kind of a trade, you know? Learn something where they can sit down and not go fishing or logging all the time. That's the way they do it nowadays – logging and fishing. Hardly anybody sitting in the office, you know – well educated. We don't have that and I'm fearful about it! ¶ This self-government business is going to pull us down. There are just a few who are well educated, and, if they should go, who's going to take over? I'm fearful for the people in the next generation because they're not really going to school. We have lots of young people who are not finishing school, not even high school. Some tribes have well educated people but we don't have any here. ¶ Young people are so different nowadays, completely different. Now they just go out anytime doing things they shouldn't be doing. They're so different now – we feel sorry for them. They're doing the wrong thing – some of them in jail, some drinking when they are very young, getting into alcohol. And it hurts us old people because they don't know what they're getting into. They can't seem to understand, even though they see it on TV, what happens to, you know, drug addicts and all that, alcoholics – they see it but they won't believe it: 'It's not going to happen to me.'

p. 160

CHIEF JAMES WALLAS

Born 1907. Quatsino, New Quatsino Village, BC
Parents: Billy and Jenny Wallas

I used to live in a bighouse, something like the one at Alert Bay. Used to be four families sharing that bighouse. Old couple used to live close to the door. I used to listen to them telling the stories, like in my book [*Kwakiutl Legends*]. In the old days it was different from now. Today you get in your car and go to the store – it was canoe in them days. ¶ Wallas is our family name from a long time ago, maybe 2,000 years ago. I'll tell you a little story of how I got this name. Cape Scott, our people used to live there a long time ago. The Creator came and he told all the people that he came to fix those that were born blind, the crippled that can't walk, and some that can't talk. The Creator had a brother, Namugwis, similar to the Bible. 'I'm leaving here to fix up the crippled people,' he tells his brother. 'When I leave, you going to stay here until I come back. I'm gonna get some food for you.' He says to his brother, 'Let's go to the point of this island' (Cape Scott). He takes out one of those double-headed sea serpents, takes the eyeballs off it, and he uses it for a slingshot to kill a whale. When that eyeball hit the whale, the whale started swimming fast and jumped up on the beach.

He did this to four of them. We're named after this biggest one, Wallas. That's an old name, isn't it? ¶ Creator says to his younger brother, 'I'm going to give you a name, we're going to call you Namugwis because you gonna be all alone here.' That's what that name means. 'I'm going – I'm gonna leave you and go around and do my work.' He says, 'You got lots of food. I don't know how long I'm gonna be till I come back.' He starts walking, walking, walking, and he sees these blind women digging roots on the tide flats. And one of the two ladies maybe got a good nose – she says, 'Um, I smell something different.' The Creator, he just stands back and listens. 'I can't see 'em, but I'm smelling something different.' The Creator talks to her: 'It's me.' They call him by his name – his name is Qaniqila. He says, 'I'm gonna fix you, to make you see. You must be born like this,' he says. 'Ya, we born like this.' He smooths their eyes with his fingers and they start to see. 'Uh, now I see a man, I see the mountains, water. I never seen before.' Then he goes walk, walk again. He comes to this man, he says, 'Were you born like you are now?' He says, 'Yes.' He had a hundred mouths all over. All answered the same word. Creator says, 'I'm gonna fix you, so you have one mouth, like me.' He smooths his body all over with his hands. 'Now you're fixed – you only got one mouth,' Creator says. I used to wonder if he had to feed 'em all – must be! ¶ He starts walking again, and he sees two men. One of them throws down a rock and says, 'I'm a greater man than everybody.' The other guy picks up the rock and says the same thing, 'I'm greater than everybody.' The Creator asks him, 'Why are you different than everybody? Men are all the same.' They stop, look, and wonder, who is this man? Never seen him before, never heard him talk like that. He tells them, 'There is no greater, all men are the same.' They found out who he was. Then he walks again, and he walks and walks and he sees this man standing on the beach looking down. Creator says to him, 'Why you standing here looking down?' The man answers him, 'Ain't you heard what we heard? We heard somebody gonna come along and fix a man, cure a sick man, a blind man. We heard this – he's gonna come.' The Creator says, 'That's me.' The Creator didn't like his answer. They never say what it was, but he didn't like it. He says: 'You not gonna be a man any more, you gonna be turned into a rock. You gonna still be standing here.' Just that minute he turned into a rock. I once took a picture of that rock. He leaves him there. He finds this man who is sharpening a spear on a rock. And the Creator asks him what he is making. He says the same thing as the man before. 'Haven't you heard a man is coming? I'm making a weapon. If he's rough on us, I'm gonna use this spear.' The

Creator says 'Let take a look at it.' He hands it over to him. He looks, looks, and looks. He says, 'Okay, you turn around and face the other way.' This man turns around, and Creator takes the weapon he made and jabs it right on his behind here. And that's a tail now – he turned into a deer. He takes that powder that they use when they sharpen weapons, and he tells him to turn around the other way. When he turns around the other way, he smears it on the other side, and he says, 'You gonna be a deer all your life.' The Creator finds a man standing on the middle of his canoe, singing. The Creator hears, and he listens, trying to catch on to what they are singing about. And he says, 'Don't anybody come near me. You are a different man than I am.' Creator comes out from the woods where he was hiding, and he says, 'Come on over to the shore – I want to talk to you.' This man comes over to the shore, and he asks him what he is singing for. 'Oh I'm singing about this good weather.' It was a good sunshine day. Creator says, 'Come over closer to me.' Creator gets hold of him and puts him in the water. 'You gonna be a rat fish – not gonna be a man any more. Go ahead, swim. You gonna live in the water, not on the land any more.' ¶ The Creator came back to Cape Scott, and he see his younger brother lying there – nothing but bones. It must have taken a long time to go walking around the world. He talks to his brother before he does something. He says, 'You think you're dead, you just sleep.' He takes a sprinkling of water and gets up back to flesh again. His younger brother rubbing his eyes says, 'Gee I'm a long time asleep, I guess.' 'You weren't asleep – you nothing but bones,' Creator tells him.

p. 138

LOUISE WATTS

Born 1914. Ohiat, Port Albion
Parents: Harry and Louise Mountain

THE biggest change I've seen is that today Native people don't like working! They want to sit at home and get money from welfare. When I was young everybody had to work for themselves. You know how much we used to get up here weeding farms? Thirty-five cents an hour! It was hard work. My oldest boy is fifty-four now, and I used to pack him and we'd go to work. I'd lay him under a little tree where it's shady, and we'd work right from 8:00 AM to 5:30 PM. ¶ It's very good for grandparents to raise children. I've raised my two grandsons – that's the traditional way. The children can understand more, and you can discipline them. The kids were small when they came with me, now they're good workers. They know how to run the farm. When they come home they pack the wood in, feed the animals, and care for everything that needs fixing. Nowadays they got everything. I tell you, the modern woman, pretty soon they will just push a button and a man will come to the bedroom! ¶ I was six when I went to residential school – stayed there until I was fourteen. It was a good experience. We had half a day of school, and then they showed us how to do things. When I grew up I knew how to crochet and all that. When I was about twelve years old, me and this other woman used to go downstairs and cook for 200 kids. The teachers, they treated us really good. They had us in shifts – half day of school, half day of work. ¶ Today, bingo's got the women – bingo halls! Every day, every afternoon, every night, even Sundays. I don't know what the difference would be if you were drinking, except you don't get a hangover. I think you're wasting your money. Imagine, the smoke in there all day long! ¶ In March the spring salmon comes in. They'd go up the river until they had all their fish dried for the winter. There was a big smoke-house where the dam is now. All the people would live in it, maybe three to four couples. There was beds around on the floor and a fire sitting in the middle, maybe two. Anybody that woke up would put another stick of wood in it. ¶ The young people today, I tell them to eat the food we used to eat. There's lots of food in the canal, they don't have to live up here where the beer parlour's next door. You know, pizza and all that stuff. Go down to the canal – you'll live longer.

p. 126

ELLEN WHITE
Born 1922. Nanaimo, Nanaimo, BC
Parents: Charles and Hilda (Bob) Rice

WE lived on a little island [when I was young]. My grandfather, George Rice, was from Skagit County and my grandmother, Mary, was from Kuper Island. He didn't feel welcome on Kuper Island so they bought this little island – they had a little money. It is registered as Norway Island, but everybody knows it as Rice Island. They were there for ten years or so, and they found that they had to pay taxes. Since he was from the States, and since he was not 'status' and not a Canadian, he became sort of an immigrant. And so we were non-status Indians. There was a school on Kuper Island, a residential school – Catholic. We were not allowed to go there because we were non-status Indians. One of the sisters was very kind – she would let us sit on the balcony and copy the work. Since my brother Russell was adopted (Indian adoption) by my grandpa Tommy, he was able to go to the school. We used to sit on the balcony, but the priest kept kicking us out. We wanted to learn so badly, so when my brother came home he had homework for us. In the meantime, granny said, 'Since you're not going to school, you're *going* to go to school.' So

Ellen White

quite a few of us went to school her way – learning how to be a midwife, herbalist, and energy communicator. I started that when I was very young. I didn't know she was doing it to a few of us until she asked me to go with her. She told me, 'I'm going to take you to a friend of mine. She owes me something and you're gonna be very good. You're gonna help me – we're gonna deliver her baby.' I was only nine, and I thought, 'I can't do it. I've never seen how it is done.' And she said, 'You have been learning all these years. Remember that little story, and that other story, and that? OK, we're just going to follow that.' And when I finally got there everything just seemed to fit like a jigsaw puzzle. ¶ A lot of things happened when I was nine. I shot my first deer. I was the eldest one of the family at home – brother Russ was away. The eldest sisters were married, and my father was ailing, so he taught me his way, which is the male side of the family's way. So I was taught by both female and male. Father taught me and Grandpa Tommy took over. I knitted my first sweater at nine. I spun the wool – [the sweater was] a grotesque looking thing. My cousin Johnny loved it – he said he did. That was a turning point in my life. When I was writing my story, as I'm still doing, so many things came about. I thought, 'Did I do that, did that happen to me?' To the best of my ability, I learned – because the old people said you must. To keep the old people alive within, you must

learn, because how else are the words going to be passed on to the next generation, and the next, and so on. That is the only way, so I did. I learned quite well, she said. ¶ There were times the training was quite difficult – water training, for example. I didn't like water too much. During water training you are put in water – you walk underneath water. That was a little difficult – sometimes during training you hate your elder. I loved both my grandmothers and grandpa Tommy, but their cousins, their method – they didn't have that love my grandparents had, it seemed like. But they were good teachers. I hated them, but to this day I still say thank you when I use whatever they taught me, such as when I'm counselling people, especially sick people. It's difficult to tell [about the teachings] because it would be giving away the training, and there's always a danger, they said. Even today, I heard this at a justice [elders advisory] meeting: 'If we tell and keep on talking about the very secret and sacred methods that we were shown, it might deplete the energies that we receive from it.' The energies we receive are not for ourselves, usually, but for the people we are working on. So there's always a danger, my grandparents told me. So it's been passed on – passed on generation after generation. I just heard an elder talk about this, not in English. He revealed to us what had happened and the experiences he had, and showed that he had lost whatever he was looking for by talking about it. I was always told that if you have visitations from the spirit world you shouldn't talk about it until you are certain that visitation was meant to help you. ¶ My Indian education sort of stopped a bit when I was ten or so, and my father was getting worse – his heart wasn't very good. Going to Ganges, getting tested and all that, going to Duncan. It was when we were going to Ganges that they found out we were supporting ourselves by digging clams, fishing, and my mother making sweaters to sell. Other monies, no. All the monies my mother and father were trying to gather were almost depleted by this time. When they asked him how we were surviving, he said: 'The kids fish and we sell the fish. They dig clams and sell them.' So the concern came from the government people, and they said, 'Does this man qualify for some sort of help?' So they gave us so much a month to help. I remember the great big side of bacon a month – a whole side, and a sack of flour. And I remember four tins of baking powder, and we always had these buckets of lard and two buckets of Roger's syrup. We always had a bucket of molasses because dad said molasses was very good for us, and we had a sack of rice. I always remember some of the rice they sent had little worms in it. So we would dump all the rice and go through it one by one – every one. But we spent the time because we liked rice. ¶ By this time they said we must have some form of education, since we were off the reserve and we weren't status. There was another island, Reed Island – it had a little herring processing plant, and we used to trade there. They [provincial government] said they were going to build a school there for us and they built us a house – a little house. It was one large room, and when my brother came home he put a little bedroom at the back. We helped our late brother build the house. When we finally built the house and were gonna move in, we found out they didn't have any money to build a school. There was no money at all, but there was a boat-house belonging to Domingo Silvy, and he said we could use that. So we used the boat-house – we cleaned it out, we put a stove in there. They brought the desks from Ganges, Salt Spring Island, and around there – old desks that had to be bolted down onto the floor. Of course they didn't have any money for the flooring, so there was just the original floor on it, and when the tide came in you could see the water underneath it. When it was blowing too hard it would just bubble right at your feet. For the longest time we had to row from our island to Reed Island, even in a storm. My father would sit all the time on the other side of our island, facing Reed Island, to see that we got there, and he knew when we were coming home. We always said that if we tipped he couldn't do anything anyway. But he said that with his strength, with his mind, we would be all right. That's what he wanted to send us, that's what he wanted – to be with us, because he was very strong in mind and was a very spiritual man. I wasn't quite fourteen when my dad died, and it really broke up the family. My mother was a very quiet lady, and we always thought she was a saint because she never drank, never swore, never smoked, never got mad. We always used to try and get her very angry, so she could hit us and maybe come out of her shell. But she never did. ¶ Before my father died, we used to hunt for lynx and racoons and the like. Somebody gave him a little canoe – it just fit him. It must have been maybe ten or twelve feet long – very narrow, very light, very swift. We'd tie anything that we had with us – like the paddle or guns. You had your carbine, always had it in a pouch – we always had it tied to our bodies. And with the headgear and the flints that we used to put the light on, we'd hunt at night. At that time, the fisheries [DOF], we knew just where they were going to be at certain times, and we would avoid that area. When we dried the skins we'd have them in the attic. We always wanted to build stairs but we never did – we always had a ladder. Even if we used it as a sleeping quarter we'd use the ladder. But during the day the ladder wouldn't be there, and the top would be completely closed. If they should come into the house, these fisheries people, they wouldn't

see it. Dad used to train us a lot, and grandpa would train us to be comfortable with water. You can do anything in water. And even if you're soaking wet and it's winter, you can be comfortable – because you just say, 'I'm going to be comfortable.' We were going along and we heard this sound, and he said, 'Can you hear it?' I said, 'Yes, I can.' It was a bump, bump, bump. It was the motor of the 'man with the iron hand.' He didn't have a hand below his elbow – he had an iron hand, like. He was the government man who watched things and charged Indians if they were caught – 'poaching' I guess, was the word. He said, 'The bay.' We were speaking Indian. So I just pushed my paddle. He was in the back and we turned upside down. You had to know every niche in every rock where you could have a foothold or protection so they wouldn't see you on the boat if they were putting their light onto shore. A lot of times there'd be a log there, and you'd be happy if the light was there because you'd just go behind the log. But this time there was just the rock. The canoe, if it was upside down, would look like a log – they always scraped the bottom of the canoe so it looked just like a log. All of a sudden he said, 'We're gonna tip it.' And you had to know just which side he was gonna do it, according to where you were closest to the shallowest spot and according to the way the rocks came down from the hills. You had to hold the canoe in the middle and never mind the paddle and guns because you knew they were tied anyway. You had to sort of push the canoe up as you tipped instead of having it on its side or you would lose that air [inside]. You had to try and touch bottom, and if you couldn't touch bottom you could still breathe in the bottom of the canoe. We stayed, and you could really hear the propeller, until he was gone. ¶ To be an elder you first have to be accepted, listened to, and not laughed at. You have to be a good speaker, relaxed – you can always say something funny to make them laugh. You're not nervous – they say if you're nervous you're looking for what you're gonna say. On the spot, when somebody puts you on the spot, you've already got this prepared speech – you just grab it out of your head. They always say when you have your teachers on both sides of you you're gathering knowledge. You always know where its going to be in your memory, in your mind. It's so easy to just go into that – they always mention a basket and you know its all in there. You can't make the same kind of speech at a funeral as you do at a wedding, or a naming, or for honouring the dead. So you have to know where all these speeches are. It was grandpa's job to train – he was a lodgehouse speaker. They did a lot of, shall we say, almost like 'plays' – they'd tell you to make a speech about something. You had to make a speech about it.

They didn't tell you to stand and be rigid when you were small, they just told you to do it. You could play with your toes, play with the ground, play at whatever you were doing and still make a speech. You could be knitting and like that. The more you did that the more you became, shall we say, qualified. You were aware of what you were doing by doing it. That made the elders very happy. ¶ If you're gonna be a midwife, you have to know medicine. You have to know how to speak with the women. You have to know the system of communication to communicate with the energy within the fetus. You have to have a very visual energy. You can instantly rerun things in your mind. You have to become good at analyzing and knowing what it is you're seeing. I have been doing midwifery since I was nine. I helped my mother with a few. First time I ever did anybody outside I was about sixteen years of age. I did another one right after that – a few months or so. Shyness, I think, was the thing in my mind – I was very shy. Maybe the embarrassment of a person made me embarrassed. Or maybe showing my embarrassment made *them* embarrassed. Talking with the grandmothers and others like that, they said that they were the same, but the more you do it, the easier it becomes. You go and keep talking about what you're doing, what you want them to do – you can't just talk about the weather. You must make them feel comfortable and make them take a journey. They become somebody else, they don't feel that they are themselves. It's another level of energy, that's what makes it easy. Once you do that, then you become very comfortable. ¶ It [Elders Justice System Advisory] has been going on for two years. It started with adoption and placement of babies. The judge's finding was: 'Who knows better, who can look after these babies better than the old people?' If they cannot look after them, they can at least suggest somebody. They can talk to these people, make these people believe that they can raise this child to the best of their abilities, just like their own children. People didn't want to do that in case somebody said they were not raising that child properly, that they were spanking the child. When it happened once and it worked very well, the judges and adoption agencies came to realize that these children did not have to be adopted out only to relatives – they could be cared for by others. If people want to adopt the child, the judges could say: 'You're going to raise this child for maybe six years, ten years. And if it's from another village, let the parents have visitations.' In the summer it might be placed in their care. You always direct them to teach their history and culture. The children should never forget that each area is different from the other – that their culture is different, their ways are different, their religion is different. Belief systems are very different in different areas.

When we work it out ourselves, both sides of the families must agree, then bring in the person who was suggested – almost like the arranged marriage, when they talked about it by proxy first to see how the other person felt about it, and then brought the whole group together. Then the lawyer comes in and takes them [papers] away, and, if the judge approves them, and he usually does, that's it. ¶ To young people my grandparents always said, 'You'll do all right if your hands are both full to overflowing.' One hand could be filled with the knowledge of the White man and the other could be filled with the knowledge of your ancestors. You could study the ancestors, but without a deep feeling of communication with them it would be surface learning and surface talking. Once you have gone into yourself and have learnt very deeply, appreciate it, and relate to it very well, everything will come very easily. They always said that if you have the tools of your ancestors and you have the tools of the White man, his speech, his knowledge, his ways, his courts, his government, you'll be able to deal with a lot of things at his level. You'll not be afraid to say anything you want. A lot of people keep back – they say, 'Oh, I might hurt them – I might say something.' When your hands are both full with the knowledge of both sides, you'll grow up to be a great speaker, great organizer, great doer, and a helper of your people.

p. 174

LUCY WILLIAMS

Born 1901. Nisga'a, New Aiyansh, BC
Parents: John and Elisa Nass

YEARS ago in the old village, when I was growing up, my people talked to me, advised me in our own language. I could listen and understand what they were saying, but today I can't talk to the children or try to advise them. They don't speak our language, and they lose out a lot on our culture. When there was a gathering or feast in the old church a few years back, the speaker or the chief spoke and everybody listened to what he had to say, the advice he was giving, and they'd follow it. Not today. When the chief starts making speeches [in Nisga'a], the young men start leaving the hall on account of the English language. A few years ago the teachers forbade the children to use our language in school – it was almost like breaking the law. That generation started to use English at home, all the time. ¶ I feel we were better off when I was a child. My dad was a great hunter. He would sell fur in the fall and winter, and he always had money. We were pretty much self-sufficient – we built our own homes, built everything ourselves. There was no help from the government until 1978, when they started getting some money for food from welfare. Years ago

people pretty well looked after themselves, and I feel they were better off. The treatment of government now – they pick on the Indians in a lot of ways. They watch the Indians, what they are doing. They are good in other ways. That's the reason I have money now – old-age pension from the government. ¶ The big difference between what they did in the old days [and what] they [do now is that then they] made plans, gave advice, and put up public works. They didn't get any old-age pension or any welfare, but they always had money in their dresser. Public works is where one whole household would feed all the people that worked on the church or any building. They built the village on public works. Everybody worked free. The community took turns putting up the public works feast. They fed the people early in the morning, fed them at lunch time, and fed them at supper time. And the next day a different house did that. That's how they built the church, the gymnasium, the village, and the sidewalks – through public works. The ladies raised money – they bought the windows and doors for the church. Nowadays nobody works that way. If somebody called a public works today nobody would come because they wouldn't get paid. ¶ I was born and raised at Giplaxt'aamiks, and we went to Fishery Bay – the eulachon camp where everybody gathered. Springtime, when eulachons come around, that's where I got married. It went

Lucy Williams

p. 124

sideways quite a ways from the way things were when I was growing up to the way they are now. When I was growing up, on Saturday all the men would get all the wood ready and get prepared so they didn't have to do anything on Sunday – Sunday is a sabbath day. Nobody cuts wood, does any work, nobody goes hunting – everything would be done Saturday. Every Sunday the church was full, even children were there because they prepared for it Saturday. There are two churches here, Anglican and Church Army – same organization. In the morning the church is full for Anglican service, and in the afternoon the bell would ring and the church is full again for Church Army. In the evening, Anglican service is held and the church is full again. It's going backwards very far – Sunday they are having bingo elsewhere, and people are going to bingo. Out of the whole village only about six go to church. Church Army, today they don't hardly exist – they don't even ring the bell any more. One of the drastic changes I've seen, people [no longer respect] religion the way they used to before the road was in. Only thing I see that is going to help the people is to go back and respect religion. If they forget how we were brought up, what we based our foundation on years ago, we'll have trouble.

CHIEF ALAN WILSON
Born 1946. Haida, Massett, BC
Parents: Augustus and Grace Wilson

MY chieftainship came from my uncle. I guess he had talked it over with my mother quite a few years ago. He is still around but his health is not good. I became chief five years ago. It was a few years before that when my mother, uncle, and a couple of aunts got together and discussed it and selected me to be successor. But I wouldn't know about it for quite a few years – they didn't approach me. I guess they were just watching me to see how I acted in the community – to see if I'd be good or bad as a chief. I must have been OK because they asked [me to be chief] about a year before I potlatched. We prepared for it, and it was really quite a nice occasion. To me it was incredible. What we did was to gather together quite a few things and give away as much as we could. It was quite expensive. A few days before the potlatch I talked it over with my family. My uncle had been saving $50.00 a month to buy my truck – putting it aside. He only had a pension. He hadn't come with any money and I was holding the truck for him. The day before I got the registration transferred to him, and at the potlatch I gave him the keys to the truck. He was really happy with that. He drove it for quite some time. At the potlatch there was people from all over the place, all along the Coast, that came to attend. There was traditional singing and dancing. To me it meant so much. Two of my aunts and my sister put the chief's blanket and headdress on me. It's like the taking away of the old and putting on of the new. They took off my old blanket and headdress and put on the new one. I have seen that done several times at potlatches I have attended. After that, there was dancing and gift-giving. I can't even remember what all was given away. I bought a hundred knives to give away to the men. I got some eulachon grease from Greenville and we distributed it in several cases of jars. We divided it and passed it to all the people. ¶ The chieftainship goes from uncle to nephew. It's always the nephew on the sister's side. I have quite a few nephews and two sisters, so I just keep my eye on my nephews on my sisters' side. I just see what they're like, and I don't know but that in three, four, or five years maybe I'll potlatch again and name my successor. But right now I'm just watching them. I told them at one time that sooner or later someone would have to come after me. We have no choice in the matter, 'cause time moves on – it waits for nobody. ¶ I think people are beginning to realize now the responsibilities of a hereditary chief. They're starting to acknowledge it, as our culture takes hold again. As the culture is taking hold again among the tribes all along the Coast, people are beginning to realize the value of our elders, of our hereditary chiefs, and what has to be done in our villages. I myself am learning all the time about what a hereditary chief does and the value of a hereditary chief. I don't see myself as an elder yet because there are many that are before me that are senior people in the village. I don't know if it's because of the position I hold as a member of the RCMP or because of the way I present myself that quite a few people come to me for advice. Some of them are senior to me, and some are elders. They come to me and ask me, 'What should I do?' We talk about it, and I think because of my having listened to previous elders that I have taken on some of their knowledge. This is quite valuable to me as a person, as a hereditary chief, and as a member of the RCMP. That's why I always tell people of the valuable knowledge that our elders have. I've had the honour of speaking to many elders, and they've told me of certain things that have to be done and of the responsibilities of a person in my position. There are things I have to go to. Potlatches by different chiefs – if there's an invitation, I have to honour it. No matter what it is, whether it's a memorial dinner, wedding, whatever it might be, it's my position to go there as a leader of the village. I've spoken to people that are in political positions and we've discussed certain issues. In our Haida Nation what they want to do is get hold of our hereditary chiefs and start to use them like they've done before. It is a pretty high position, a really valuable position, and we must make use of it. I think things are going to start to change, hopefully in the very near future, concerning our hereditary chiefs. They're going to have a lot more say in a lot of things, instead of being symbolic heads, as it were, as maybe the White society sees us. Instead of being just symbolic heads, we should have a real solid part in everything. We should not just be there when the crunch is on, but be behind it right from the beginning, be the meat of the source. I think that is really important. ¶ As a hereditary chief, people watch, no matter what position you're in. Once you're in a position of responsibility, people watch you, and they watch you close, to see what you do. Not only with hereditary chiefs but with everyone. They say, 'He does this, why can't I ?' That's why you're to watch your every step, because not only your two eyes are seeing where you step but others are too. They listen to what you say, so a person in any position of authority has to be very careful, has to watch where he walks, has to listen to what he says. Not only do other people have to listen to him, but he has to listen to himself. Be very careful – you have to think about what you're gonna say. How will it affect this person or that person? How

can we bring something out that will benefit not only here but over there as well. Things we do here in the Haida Nation are really important to other people, just as things that other tribes do are important to us. That's the important thing about unity. Working together – there's so much more power in it. When you start working toward a goal, it's so much easier to have someone with you that has the same ideas, the same values. Maybe it's one, maybe it's two, maybe it's a clan, and maybe it's a whole tribe working together. For example, think of Lyle Island, South Moresby – the Skidegate Haida and the Massett Haida worked together and something was accomplished. We found how much more can be accomplished through working together rather than having internal conflicts. Get those out of the way. If we can work together as a unit and intertwine with the unit to the south, which is Skidegate, we can all work as one and there's no stopping us. ¶ This canoe trip to Alaska this past week – I had the honour of being part of that. To me it was an incredible voyage. In my view that voyage symbolically shattered that boundary that the U.S. and Canadian governments have put between us and our friends and relatives of the Haida Nation to the north. When we paddled across there, there were paddlers from Massett, Skidegate, and Haidaburg, and we all worked together going across. It was just incredible. When we left here it was dark, coming past the village. I know many people were still sleeping – it was 3:30 in the morning. We came past here, and the feeling of someone watching us was incredibly strong. It sent a chill right up my spine and I think the others felt it. We passed here and got to the outside, and one of the paddlers said, 'We should pray.' So we stopped paddling and asked God for guidance and mercy on our trip. It was absolutely incredible going across – we could see Alaska: our destination was set. We continued to paddle and all I could think of was our ancestors and how they did that. They never had escort boats or anything, but we were doing something that hasn't happened in about one hundred years, going across that water to the Dixon Entrance to visit our friends and relatives in Haidaburg. Everybody talked about that border – it wasn't visible but it was there. Yet those two canoes shattered it symbolically. It was a line that was there before, but it is gone now because we took it away. ¶ As we came around the point into Haidaburg the chill just started all over. It must have been seventy degrees Fahrenheit. It was warm, not a breeze, a beautiful day – yet the chill went right from my head through my body, and the hair stood up on my arm. I turned to Woodrow Morrison, who is from Haidaburg, and I said, 'It feels as if I've been here before.' As we were paddling along the feeling was incredible. This is what our ancestors did! Ernie Colinson was seated behind me, and he said later that he seen the chill coming up my arms and my hair standing up, and tears started to roll. Oh, it was just incredible! The people on the beach were there to greet us – I don't know how many there was. I don't know – 1,000 maybe 1,300 people, but the beach was just full. Wow! It was just absolutely incredible, and I can't even find words to describe what was happening within me! It was almost like something in the past had come back and just took a grasp on us. Maybe it was a feeling that our ancestors were happy with what we were doing. There was more to it than we could really see, and that's how the people on the beach felt. They said the feeling when we came around the point was just – people couldn't speak. When we came up one of our chiefs spoke to the chief from Haidaburg, and when that canoe turned and touched the beach it felt complete. ¶ I think that's what unity is – knowing one another and coming together and working with no conflict within. In that way, if anything opposes us that conflict can be transferred to them and make our battle easier. That's what unity is. That's what I feel. We're going to have to transfer that unity to all the tribes along our Coast. As a Native people, as an Indian people, we have to work together. I think we can be stronger – we can help lift one another – we can be a unit. Our numbers might be small but we can be bigger than the forces that oppose us if we work as a unit. I think that's how battles were won too. Today our battle is a battle of words, between us and our opposition, whoever that might be. I think if we took all the knowledge of our elders along with the knowledge of our young people, who have educated themselves, and put them together, nobody could stand ahead of us no matter who it might be. That's really important. Our elders are important, our young people are really important – that's our future. So if we can take what our young people have to offer us with their knowledge of today, take the knowledge of our elders with their knowledge of yesterday, and combine those two things, we have something to hand on to our young people's children and their children's children. It's powerful – that's what unity is, right there. I think that unity starts within ourselves – we have to want it. I want our future generations to say, 'We have this because my father, my mother, my grandfather, my grandmother fought for it, and we have it.' I don't want to see my grandchildren or my great grandchildren fighting for what we're fighting for today. I want them to be established. We have a positive outlook, and, working together, it can be done. ¶ I joined the RCMP on July 26, 1976. At that time, and even now, there was a lot of conflict between Native society and White society – not only here

but throughout BC and Canada. And I felt that I should help in some way. Then this opportunity to become a policeman came along, so I joined as an auxiliary member for two years. I put in my application for the Native special constable program, and in 1976 I signed on the dotted line in Prince Rupert. I really wouldn't trade my job for anything. There was one fella, he was in the wrong place at the wrong time. I don't know if it was due to the influence of friends or what. I had a talk with him and I've never had to deal with him again. I like to think that if I can help one fella like that, instead of having him going to court every other month or jail every other year, it makes it all worthwhile. I've worked in my own village here for thirteen years and I've never really had any problem. I've talked to other fellows that have gone into the RCMP and heard the problems that they have had in their own home towns. Sometimes it is hard to believe. People have accepted me in my position as both policeman and hereditary chief. It makes me have to tread a lot more lightly than others do. ¶ If I could speak to a young person who has, or is getting an education, I would advise him to speak with the elders and to listen. Listening is so important. There's a wealth of knowledge you can get from our elders – they can't teach it at school. To a young person I guess an elder really doesn't have to be an old person – it could be myself, it could be anybody. I'd advise

p. 170

young people to complete their education in this system that we're facing now and to speak to our elders. That would make a solid foundation for them, and then they could reach out a little bit further. They would have their roots, which are solid, deep, and strong as well as a White education. I think that is what I would tell young people.

CHIEF ERNIE AND WINNIE YELTATZIE

Born 1906 and 1902. Haida, Massett, BC
Parents: Alec and Agnes Yeltatzie
Henry and Martha Edenshaw

IT was good in the village when we were young, not like these days. There was dances all the time, and some of us girls and my sisters would go to all the dances. Everybody just had a good time – no drinking or anything. It used to be really good. We never used to run around like other girls – we just used to stay home. We were used to it – we never used to go out. ¶ Before we got married, I used to work in a sawmill – I was sixteen years old. I started before I was sixteen. It was a great big sawmill. I also ran a tugboat for a while, and after that I started fishing. When we got married [1925], we moved down to North Island in a little trolling boat. We were going so fast, Winnie got scared the bottom was going to drop out of the boat. We were in that boat for ten days. The money sure used to be scarce. We moved over here to cut spruce during the war. There was a big flu here then, in 1918. I didn't get it [Winnie] because I was staying in Massett with my sisters, and none of us got sick. Gee, everybody was dying down here, and in Massett nobody got the flu. I don't know how that was. Our doctors weren't very good, like now. There was hardly any doctors. Lots of people died.

The same thing happened in Haidaburg – a first cousin of ours and quite a few others died. They used to have a funeral every day. ¶ My grandfather [Ernie] was a canoe builder, that's how he made his living. That's all he did all his life – build canoes. He used to take me out to Port Simpson, where he used to take his canoes and trade for all kinds of things – anything he could get hold of. He used to take it to the Tlingit coast and sell his things – that's how he used to make his money. I [Winnie] just remember one canoe – those old people living back here used to have a big canoe and they'd go out in it. In the summertime we used to borrow it sometimes and go berry picking with mother. ¶ They never used to teach us [Ernie] in school – the teacher used to sit down and read the newspaper all day. We'd all sit around there all day with our books. The teacher was there, but they never used to teach us. They said they weren't allowed to teach Indians because they took all the country away from us, and they know we'll make a fuss over it – so they never teach us. We never had a chance to go to school. If I'd had a chance to go to school, I bet I'd have been smart. When I came over here, I tried going to school, but it was no use, I couldn't learn anything - it was the teacher. When I was fifteen there was one teacher that noticed that I [Winnie] was learning good, so she had me sit in front of all the desks to teach me more. Two old guys wanted to take the job and they got her fired. They started teaching, and I went to school one day. He made me write down something, and I wrote it all out in no time. And I quit school – what's the use in going when I know more than him? They said he was laughing. He said, 'I give Winnie something to do and she writes down all the answers in no time. She knows more than I do.' So I couldn't go – fifteen years old and I couldn't go any more. I went to residential school for awhile – that school was just for half-breeds. I don't know why they did that [special mixed-blood school]. Father tried to put Jeffery in there too, but they wouldn't take him. Father had to pay so much a month for school. They used to have boys' and girls' schools then for all the Indians. ¶ People [Winnie] used to behave better in those days. Now that they're educated they're acting so crazy around here – lots of drinking and everything. When we first came here they didn't allow Whites to come into the reservation. Mr. Teasey, he was the Indian Agent, if anybody White came down here he'd look after them. If they stayed too long, he'd tell them, 'Go.' My father [Winnie] became a Canadian citizen and he stopped it – he worked hard to get Teasey out of it. Mr. Teasey was a strict old man. When we [Ernie] first came over here and started getting a reservation, we had a hard time. We were American citizens from Haidaburg, Alaska. Father [Winnie] had to work hard a long time to get us placed here. One thing my father did good was to bring the family over here from Haidaburg to be baptized. That's one thing that helped them. They asked him, 'Why do you want to move over here?' He said, 'I had all my children baptized right here in this church.' ¶ When we were young there were no potlatches – they're just starting that lately. For a long time there used to be potlatches, but the preachers stopped that. They made them cut down all the totem poles – there used to be lots here. They thought that the poles were their idols – they wasn't. They didn't pray to them. It was just like a big potlatch when they used to raise a totem pole.

p. 130

CHIEF NATHAN YOUNG
Born 1919. Haida, Skidegate, BC
Parents: Mark and Louise Young

I took after my uncle on my mother's side – that's where I get my chieftainship. You always take after your mother's footsteps – that's how it works with the Haida. You're born and raised for it from the time you're a baby – they don't just point you out and have you be chief. You got to know history about different things – that's why when you're growing up the old people will tell you different stories. The toughest part, when I was growing up, was when I was made to know I was going to be chief. I was still quite a young boy yet, because my clan was dying off. There wasn't too many of us left. There was quite a few of us, but they kept dying off – there was a big flu before. That took the count of the Haidas down to nothing. At the time the tribes moved over to Skidegate, they figured the count at 10,000. That's on this end [South Island]. That's not counting Massetts. It's something awful! It got down to 200 people for a long time. We're up to about 600 or 700 people now, I guess. They're coming back – our community is getting bigger. This winter there're twenty houses coming in. That's the way things are going now. ¶ I was told I had to do what

I was told by my uncle – he taught me and brought me out to our country. That man used to say when we were out, 'Our beautiful country' – that's the way he used to put it. He'd say, 'My goodness, how beautiful! Just look around!' He'd say, 'One of these days,' (this is all in our language) 'maybe in your time you won't see any trees here – they'll all be gone. It's going to be all logged off.' This was in 1918, when they weren't taking wood out that fast. Just look how far ahead that man looked to see the way logging was going to go. He wasn't that far off. ¶ We'd go along and he'd tell me every point has a name – it's called such and such. 'That island, nephew, it's got a name,' and he tells you that one too. Now you got to memorize all those god darned names! Well, it's not an easy thing, eh? He started on me too late. First trip we were gone for a week – did a little seal hunting and what not. He'd tell me different stories about things that went on years ago. I'd take it in – try to memorize it. When we got home my stepmother would say, 'Did you learn anything?' I said, 'He told me a lot – the names of the country.' She said, 'That's the idea.' ¶ He said to me, 'I hope you'll be ready to take the name Tanu when I'm gone – I haven't got that much time left.' When my uncle passed on, the family held a meeting to see who would hold the name. I never had nothing to say – I was too young. They decided this guy that was older than me would take the name over until I got old enough, which is legal – it's been done. Even if I get old enough I don't dare touch it because he's in the same clan. When he passed away, we didn't take the name over right away – we had a big pot-latch for the chief, and we left the name open for a year. I'm married to my uncle's daughter – that's the real Haida way, the tradition from before. One evening, we're sitting in the house, had a nice fire going, and there's a knock on the door. There's an old lady there, and a man – three or four of them. I tell them in Haida, 'Come in, sit down.' I'm a bit keyed up - you don't see them elders like that. After awhile one of the women start talking to me, leading up to it. One of the men says to me, 'Are you ready to take the name over?' He says, 'Its your place. You know it and we don't want you to wait any longer. We want you to do it right now.' My God, they didn't even ask me if I had money or anything for that! Just like that, bang! Money was scarce, damn scarce, eh? 'Right now. Next week if you can do it.' Holy cow, what am I gonna do? But I can't say no – they're the boss. 'If you leave it too long the name will die off. We've seen it before, we don't want to see it again.' Okay, I said to the wife, Mrs. Young, 'What's gonna happen? I guess we're gonna starve this winter.' She looked at me and said, 'When we got married we didn't have nothing anyway. We got by and I guess we'll do it again.'

Well, by golly, that was the best answer in the world! ¶ I told 'em, 'I'm ready, I'll do what I can. Gifts though. There're no gifts! If you'd 'a give me a little more time, I could have got lots of stuff from Vancouver.' 'That's all right, just use cash,' she said. Holy cow, I didn't have any cash! My wife's brother had a store – you can see the remains of it yet. He comes from Tanu, too. I tell him what happened: 'People come to see me – they want me to put a potlatch on right away to take your dad's name over. But the financial part – I wouldn't say I'm broke, but I'm gonna need money.' He says, 'What are you after?' I say, 'You got the store here, how much can you back me?' Them days we lived on credit – there was no money. Well, he says, 'I'll tell you what, you been a good customer. I'll go you all the ways. Take whatever you want!' 'To start with I got to have half a cow anyway, all the vegetables, the fruit. We'll have to have the women folks to figure that out.' ¶ When I got home, I tell my wife what the score is. 'Good' she says, 'the big step is over with. The next step is the cooks.' Always a head cook for different things in them days – one group specialized in the pies, one the cakes, and so on. All your relations chipped in a few dollars, too, and it was a big help – and I mean a *big* help! At the potlatch, that was the first time they sang my chief's song for me. I didn't put my regalia on because it had disap-

peared when the chief had passed away. The regalia was passed on from hand to hand – your cape and your headpiece. I did what I was supposed to do, and I was thanked by my public. The Haidas danced for quite a while – them days they used to really go in for it. ¶ The Haidas were easy people to get along with, meek and everything, you know. But they had that mean streak, too, I guess. They were always on a raiding party – that's something they were known for. It gave us quite a bad name with our neighbours, mostly in the Skeena area. They used to go as far as Seattle in those big canoes, like the Lootas canoe we have now. My clan, the Tanu, they were warriors – they weren't scared to die. They'd go out fighting any time. They were the warriors of the Queen Charlotte Islands, the Tanu people. ¶ First the Tanu people settled in Church Creek, named after the chief from Tanu. When he moved over to Skidegate, the chief knew he was coming. Well, he's the only chief that moved here from all these villages from all over these islands that really got a welcome. When he landed out here, Chief Skidegate came out and met Ghitkon, the chief from Tanu. He grabbed his hand and led him up. There was a house already standing here. He brought him up to the house and told him in Haida, 'All right, this is your house.' The house was all ready for him. That's the welcome he got, from one chief to the next. He had all his followers

with him. Don't take long – everybody gets busy
and they start building houses. When he got settled
he put on a feast for his community, eh? Mostly
Indian food in them days – nothing fancy. He went
down into the territory – went after seagull eggs.
They had lots of dried fish and they had seagull
eggs for dessert. That was a big potlatch, eh? He
gave gifts away, of course. They gave mostly blankets away in them days – trinkets were hard to
come by, I guess. That's how all the Haidas got all
together here in Skidegate.

PHOTOGRAPHS

∧< **CHIEF JOE MATHIAS**
Born 1943. Squamish, North Vancouver, BC
Parents: William and Elizabeth (Jacob) Mathias

∧ > **CHIEF ALAN WILSON**
Born 1946. Haida, Massett, BC
Parents: Augustus and Grace Wilson

∧ > ELLEN WHITE
Born 1922. Nanaimo, Nanaimo, BC
Parents: Charles and Hilda (Bob) Rice

∧ < **CHIEF EDWIN NEWMAN**
Born 1926. Heiltsuk/Kwagiutl, Waglisla, BC
Parents: Carey and Jessie (Anderson) Newman

∧< CHIEF NATHAN YOUNG
Born 1919. Haida, Skidegate, BC
Parents: Mark and Louise Young

131

EMMA HUNT
Born 1912. Kwagiutl, Fort Rupert, BC
Parents: Dr. Billy and Edith Nelson

GABRIEL BARTLEMAN
Born 1913. Saanich, Saanich, BC
Parents: Isaac and Martha (Irvin) Bartleman

133

∧< CATHERINE ADAMS
Born 1903. Gwa'sala'Nakwaxda'xw, Gwa'sala'Nakwaxda'xw Reserve, BC
Parents: Kenneth and Lucy Henderson

135

∧ GRACE AZAK
Born 1923. Nisga'a, Canyon City, BC
Parents: James and Lucy (Moore) Swanson

> ADELAIDE HAFFTOR
Born 1911. Lytton, Lytton, BC
Parents: George and Mary (James) Phillips

< LOUISE WATTS
Born 1914. Ohiat, Port Albion
Parents: Harry and Louise Mountain

∧ LUCY SMITH
Born 1931. Gwa'sala'Nakwaxda'xw, Gwa'sala'Nakwaxda'xw Reserve, BC
Parents: James and Ida (Seaweed) Henderson

∧< (PAST) CHIEF COUNCILLOR
RUBY DUNSTAN
Born 1941. Nl'aka'pamux, Lytton, BC
Parents: Andrew and Sarah (Blachford) Johnny

∧ > CHIEF CHARLIE (JAMES) SWANSON
Born 1921. Nisga'a, Greenville, BC
Parents: James and Lucy Swanson

CHIEF BERT MACK
Born 1924. Tuquot, Ucluelet Reserve, BC
Parents: Cecil and Jesse Mack

CHIEF ALEX FRANK
Born 1919. Clayoquot, Meares Island, BC
Parents: Francis and Effie Frank

145

∧ > CHIEF RODERICK ROBINSON
Born 1931. Nisga'a, New Aiyansh, BC
Parents: George and Pauline (Adams) Robinson

146

MARY CLIFTON
Born 1900. Sahtloot, Comox, BC
Parents: Billy and Mary Frank

MARGARET JOSEPH-AMOS
Born 1918. Clayoquot, Aesousista Reserve, BC
Parents: Tim and Lucy Manson

∧ > CHIEF CLARENCE DEMPSEY COLLINSON
Born 1928. Haida, Skidegate, BC
Parents: Dora and Adolphus Collinson

CHIEF BILL WILSON
Born 1945. Cape Mudge, Comox, BC
Parents: Charles and Ethel (Johnson) Wilson

(PAST) CHIEF ED SPARROW
Born 1898. Musqueam, Vancouver, BC
Parents: John and Matilda Sparrow

COUNCILLOR CLARENCE JULES
(Ex-Chief, Kamloops Indian Band)
Born 1926. Kamloops, Kamloops, BC
Parents: Joe and Agnes (Duncan) Jules

CHIEF SAUL TERRY
President of the UBCIC
Born 1942. Bridge River, Vancouver, BC
Parents: Nelson and Ella Terry

∧ CHIEF COUNCILLOR ALFRED HUNT
Born 1929. Kwagiutl, Fort Rupert, BC
Parents: John and Alice Hunt

> (PAST) CHIEF COUNCILLOR HARRY ASSU
Born 1905. Wewaikai, Cape Mudge, BC
Parents: Billy and Mary Assu

156

MARY HAYES
Born 1915. Clayoquot, Aesousista Reserve, BC
Parents: Johnny and Mary

AGNES THORNE
Born 1906. Halalt, Duncan, BC
Parents: Ed and Madelaine (Dick) Norris

159

∧ < CHIEF JAMES WALLAS
Born 1907. Quatsino, New Quatsino Village, BC
Parents: Billy and Jenny Wallas

< GABRIEL JACK
Born 1920. Tsawout, Sidney, BC
Parents: Peter and Emily (Thomas) Jack

∧ HENRY GEDDES
Born 1913. Haida, Massett, BC
Parents: Charles and Emma (Johnson) Geddes

SARAH TUTUBE
Born 1910. Tuquot, Port Albion, BC
Parents: Joe and Cecelia (Joe) Atzic

164

CHIEF ADAM SHEWISH
Born 1920. Sheshaht, Port Alberni, BC
Parents: Jacob and Eva Shewish

165

< **ED WILLIAMS**
Born 1894. Cowichan, Duncan BC
John and Ann (Jack) Williams

∧ **CHIEF BILL HUNT**
Born 1906. Kwagiutl, Fort Rupert, BC
Parents: Johnny and Dorothy Hunt

167

∧ < LILY SPECK
Born 1904. Tlowitsis-Mumtagila, Alert Bay, BC
Parents: Jim and Elizabeth Harry

169

∧ < **CHIEF ERNIE AND WINNIE YELTATZIE** (and grandson, Richard)
Born 1906 and 1902. Haida, Massett, BC
Parents: Alec and Agnes Yeltatzie, Henry and Martha Edenshaw

< **AGNES ALFRED**
Born 1889. Namgis, Alert Bay, BC
Parents: Gwulsalas and Puglas

∧ **HAZEL STEVENS**
Born 1900. Haida, Skidegate, BC
Parents: John and Fanny Cross

∧ LUCY WILLIAMS
Born 1901. Nisga'a, New Aiyansh, BC
Parents: John and Elisa Nass

> MARY JACKSON
Born 1906. Sechelt, Sechelt, BC
Parents: Captain George and Theresa Finchback

∧ < **BILL REID**
Born 1920. Haida, Vancouver, BC
Parents: William and Sophia (Gladstone) Reid

177

CHIEF COUNCILLOR LEONARD GEORGE
Born 1946. Burrard, North Vancouver, BC
Parents: Dan and Amy George

GRAND CHIEF JAMES SCOTCHMAN
Born 1918. Lillooet, Lillooet, BC
Parents: John and Nancy Scotchman

179

∧ < CHIEF ALVIN ALFRED
Born 1910. Namgis, Alert Bay, BC
Parents: Moses and Agnes Alfred

∧ > ETHEL ALFRED
Born 1910. Mamalilikala, Alert Bay, BC
Parents: Chief Harry and Mary Hanuse

AFTERWORD

MARJORIE HALPIN
Curator of Ethnology
UBC Museum of Anthropology

DAVID NEEL'S magnificent portrait series of British Columbia Native Chiefs and Elders reveals at a glance the rudeness, ignorance, and injustice of racism. Jarred by a moment of recognition of our own denials of the individuality and humanity of Native people, non-Native viewers must confront and transform the stereotypes that control our mind's eye into a new recognition of the particularity of the human presence. But Neel's accomplishment is not merely to confront us with the existence of stereotyping by creating its absence, he also affords us glimpses of what social intimacy is about. It just might be that social intimacy has been the 'stuff' of Native art all along, and that this is obscured to the outside world by our preoccupations with the formal continuities of design elements. ¶ David Neel was born in Vancouver in 1960 to Karen Clemenson, a non-Native, and David Neel, eldest son of Ellen Neel, the first woman carver on the Northwest Coast. Although the Neel family is Fort Rupert Kwagiutl, Ellen Neel herself was born in the house of Chief Wakas at Alert Bay, the same house that was reconstructed in 1989 in the Grand Hall of the Canadian Museum of Civilization in Hull, Quebec. David Neel's father, grandmother, and great-grandfather, Charlie James, were all carvers, as is David Neel himself. His Native name, 'T'la'lala'wis' ['a meeting of whales coming together'], was inherited from his father, who received it from his uncle, Mungo Martin. While David Neel may be the first professional photographer in the family, it is a family that has excelled in the arts of image-making for generations. ¶ Neel has drawn, since childhood, 'the same thing that I photograph now – people.' As a teenager, however, he thought his career would be in journalism, which he studied, along with Fine Arts and Anthropology, at Mount Royal College in Calgary (where his mother moved after the death of his father). He first took photographs to illustrate one of his own texts and discovered that he 'really took to it, and never looked back.' Moving to the University of Kansas, which has a famous school of photo-journalism, he learned the technical aspects of photography from his instructors and continued to study Fine Arts and Anthropology. But he learned the *art* of photography, that is, how to go beyond mere appearances, in the university's rich library of photography books and catalogues. Here he found, and still speaks with passion about, the work of Donald McCullin and W. Eugene Smith, strong independent men who followed their own visions, both of whom worked in black and white, as does Neel. Here he learned about form and style from the work of Irving Penn, who took his sitters out of their backgrounds in order to simplify his portraits to essentials. ¶ After leaving Kansas, Neel travelled and lived in Mexico for awhile, where he did a photoessay on Mexican graveyards, and discovered people whose attitudes toward the extended family and death (that it is celebrated, not denied) reminded him of his own people. He next settled in Dallas and worked for the studio of Greg Booth, where he learned the business aspects of photography by working closely with Keith Wood. Again, he was drawn to another culture in which family, place, and history were important. He spent time 'hanging out' with the residents of Freedman's Town, a community formed by slaves after the Civil War, where he was known as 'Pitcher Man,' and it was here that he developed his practice of taking prints of his photographs back to the people involved. Neel now sees this as the beginning of his commitment to collaborative projects. The Freedman's Town photographs were exhibited at Dallas's LTV Center. ¶ His next project, also in Dallas, grew out of his involvement with an inner city art community, Deep Ellum, which, like Freedman's Town, was being gentrified. He made photographs of twenty-five artists at work in their studios, and gave each artist six prints of their own photographs. The artists then incorporated Neel's photographs and their own texts about the plight of Deep Ellum into new works. The Deep Ellum show, ironically financed by the same developers who threatened the community, had a successful run at the Allen Street Gallery in Dallas. ¶ In this brief sketch of Neel's early career can be seen a number of aspects that were to flower in *Our Chiefs and Elders*: a collaborative commitment, the combination of words and images, a social consciousness, and the exploration of cultural differences. ¶ Returning to Vancouver in 1987 to set up his own commercial studio, Neel reflected upon what he had seen of the world's knowledge of his people, and slowly the idea of his next project became clear – to represent BC Native people to a naive Canadian audience all too accustomed to the stereotypes and misconceptions perpetrated by non-Native images. Aware, too, of the problems of young Natives, he saw a need for role models from Native communities. ¶ In his commercial work, Neel specializes in portraits, notably portraits of people of power and influence: company presidents, politicians, ministers, actors, artists, architects. In *Our Chiefs and Elders*, he is also photographing people of power and influence, but there the similarity ends, for the faces of power in the two worlds are very different. The following brief characterization of photographs of Native people by Outsiders puts these differences into context.

THE ANTHROPOLOGICAL LENS: Photography, 'light writing,' and anthropology, the 'science of man,' grew up together in the late nineteenth-century heyday of Western realism. The project of science, to banish unwanted human imagination or subjectivity from its descriptions of an observable reality, seemed well served by the new machine with its apparently natural production of visual facts. And there is, indeed, a direct relationship between the light reflected off objects and the resultant image of *something* there that is captured by the camera. How that something is controlled for the capture, and for what purpose, and how that image is received by a viewer, are, however, profoundly cultural matters. Victor Burgin (1982:9) refers to photographs as *catalysts* – 'exciting mental activity which exceeds that which the photograph itself provides.' ¶ Franz Boas (1858-1942), the patriarch of North American anthropology, took, in his own words, 'three watches, "Prismenkreis and Horizont," a geodetic theodolite, apparatus to measure distance and smaller ones to measure angles, a large compass, barometer, thermometer, hygrome-

ter, aneroid and a photographic apparatus' with him on his first field expedition to Baffin Island to study the Inuit in 1883 (Jacknis 1984:4). One of Boas's biographers, Ira Jacknis, writes that: 'This attitude toward instruments and recording devices – still-cameras, movie cameras, phonographs – rooted in his early training as a physicist, was to remain with Boas throughout his career.' ¶ Photography played an even greater role in Boas's subsequent work with Natives in British Columbia, beginning in 1886, as did the collecting of sketches, human measurements, crania and artefacts, plaster casts, and word lists and texts. While Boas took photographs himself, his most extensive photographic series was made in Fort Rupert in 1894 by O.C. Hastings of Victoria, a hired professional (see the analysis in Jacknis 1984). It was also probably Hastings who photographed the Natives that Boas was able to get permission to 'drag' from prison to be photographed. While Boas and other scientists of his time specialized in 'mug shots' – full face, three-quarter, and profile shots of unnamed subjects identified by tribe and supplemented by head measurements, he also took (or had taken) photographs of scenes, houses, totem poles, and activities.

THE NOBLE SAVAGE: The No-name Indian also figures prominently in the Romantic tradition, best represented by Edward S. Curtis's (1868-1952) ambitious project to photograph the Vanishing Indian 'directly from Nature' in order to create 'a comprehensive and permanent record of all the important tribes ... that still retain to a considerable degree their primitive customs and traditions' (quoted in Scherer 1985:78). To this end, Curtis travelled throughout North America photographing Natives in traditional dress and circumstances. He published these photographs in a monumental twenty-volume work, *The North American Indian* (1907-30). According to Jacknis (1984:12), Curtis 'was touched by the Pictorialist movement, which encouraged the photographer to manipulate the image to achieve a blurred, dreamy, and poetic effect – the mark of Art.' Whereas Boas and others working in the scientific tradition were resolutely anti-pictorialist and tried to keep evidence of their own personalities out of their photographs, Curtis (quoted in Lyman 1982:39) had other motives: 'Try to make your work show some individuality, or in other words, make it look yourself; let it show that you have put part of your life into it.' ¶ The romantic tradition flourished in the early years of this century, 'during which [time] the era of photographic exploration gave way to a period of documentation' (Ruby 1981:63). As in the anthropological photography tradition, the romantics controlled Native representations for their own ends. These ends are now recognized as political. Curtis,

the best-known of dozens of Romantic photographers, obtained hundreds of thousands of dollars from men like J. Pierpont Morgan to sentimentalize the 'vanishing race' (for a critical reading of Curtis, see Lyman 1982). American anthropologist, Jay Ruby (1981:49), explains:

> As western expansion caused us to come into increasingly less hostile contact with Native Americans, some people began to view them not as savages to be exterminated, or if possible converted to a civilized state, but as remnants of a 'vanishing race' whose style of life must be recorded and preserved before it goes away.
>
> *I am informed that no Indians here will consent to be photographed in a state of nudity, although reward has been offered. It is believed that they have a superstitious dread of some hidden purpose which they do not understand, and it would be impossible to explain to them the scientific object of the proceeding.* Governor Musgrave, 1870 (quoted in Schwartz 1981-82:9)

THE BEFORE AND AFTER TRADITION: Another tradition of photographing natives, Before and After photographs, deserves to be mentioned for what it reveals of the visual bias of Western thought. Most representative are some 600 known photographs taken by three different photographers for the Indian Industrial Training School, founded in Carlisle, Pennsylvania, in 1879. The Carlisle photographs show Native children from all over the United States, first, as they arrived at the school in Native dress and hairstyles and, second, as they left it 'clothed and in their right mind' (*The Valley Sentinel*, 17 October 1879, quoted in Malmsheimer 1985:57). At Carlisle, students had their hair cut short, forcibly if necessary, and were made to wear standardized Western uniforms and dresses. 'For students and their tribal parents, as for Eastern whites ... the transformation of appearance and demeanour both stood for and were part of the transformation of identity and culture' (Malmsheimer 1985:59). ¶ Outsider control and distortion of Native realities can also, of course, be recognized in both Boas's and Curtis's attempted removal of non-Native elements from their photographs in order to create a record of Native life that reflected aboriginal conditions. This attitude, that what is worth recording about Native people is that which is uncorrupted by White influence, persists today in most scientific and romantic representations. It should also be noted that these photographers work in a controlling and directorial mode, consciously and intentionally creating events, poses, and props for the camera to record. Not surprisingly, we see few smiles and little evidence of presentational energy in the subjects (or, better,

objects) of these photographs. (Renato Rosaldo's article, 'Imperialist Nostalgia,' in Rosaldo, 1989, discusses the political implications of nostalgia, as do many others, e.g., the contributors to Clifford and Marcus 1986.) ¶ Whether it is as scientists or romantics eliminating evidence of the colonizing culture's clothing, houses, picket fences, hairstyles, or the Carlisle educators' 'allegorical presentation of the "vanishing race" in the very act of disappearing' (Malmsheimer 1985:72), the assumption is that *appearances* tell the tale. That this is still so is revealed in James Clifford's (1988:284) disturbing account of the Mashpee Wampanoag Tribal Council's 1976 trial in which they had to prove that they were still, and had been continuously, Indians in order to reclaim contested lands. According to Clifford, the question at the trial was whether a jury 'could be made to believe in the persistent "Indian" existence of the Mashpee plaintiffs without costumes and props?' Predictably, they could not and the Mashpee lost. This same argument from appearances, and the denial of the right to change, was raised by the government of British Columbia in the Gitksan-Wet'suwet'en court case to claim rights over their hereditary lands (see 'The Pizza Syndrome' in Williamson 1989). ¶ We are now at the heart of racism – the stereotype – and the political realities it keeps in place. That people see Natives in terms of categories – racial types,

Noble Savages, Skid Row drunks – prevents them from seeing human beings, with all of the magnificent diversity that any population of human beings possesses. Stereotypes are essentialist and restrictive, which is why the contemporary discourse surrounding photography, especially photography of the oppressed by the powerful, is increasingly a political discourse and less and less a discourse about art. Indeed, the rights of artistic licence are being challenged. The so-called New Photographers, for example, 'reject any notion the pictures should be produced merely for one's self-satisfaction or be devoid of social comment. Instead, they analyze for ideological affiliation' (Frank Webster, quoted in Chalfen 1984:90). Outsider photographs of Natives are increasingly being interrogated as to their ideologies and purposes, and few of us can bear close scrutiny in this matter.

> The camera [became] a symbol of the oppression of Indians, as generation after generation of them had to pose for the leering cameras of weekend tourists. It is no wonder that it is hard to find a photograph of a smiling Indian before 1930. There wasn't much to laugh about when the cameras were clicking. Yet every Indian community has loads of funny stories about the tourists they had tricked, and the visitors who intruded on sacred rituals without permission, or the photographs

> which scholars published despite their claims to the contrary when they asked for permission to photograph. Stories about White photographers entered tribal oral histories and the camera became the latest weapon to be used against Indians. (Hill 1989:35)

As long as people do not control their own representations, they must, in the perverted logic of stereotyping, be representative. Conversely, as Judith Williams (quoted in Julien and Mercer 1988:4) argues, 'The more power any group has to create and wield representations, the less it is required to *be* representative.' ¶ And this returns us to a consideration of the importance of David Neel's insider portraits of Native leaders.

OUR CHIEFS AND ELDERS: Neel photographed his sitters in four different modes so as to break the viewer's essentialist mind set. He calls these the Ceremonial, the Personality, the Environmental, and the Action modes. In the Ceremonial mode, people are seen wearing the regalia and holding the symbols of rank *to which they are entitled by hereditary right*, as opposed to the earlier custom of dressing Natives in whatever traditional regalia were at hand, whether it belonged to the sitter or not. In the Personality mode, people wear ordinary clothes, and Neel's focus is on the individuality of his sitters. In the Environmental mode, people are shown in their personal surroundings. In the Action mode, community leaders are shown in their public roles. ¶ The sitters' presentational energy and obvious commitment to and enthusiasm for the project are evidence of its collaborative nature, as are the statements elicited from the sitters by the photographer. Unlike the directorial control exercised over Native poses and persons in the Outsider genres, we can see evidence of *relationship* between Neel and his sitters. Indeed, Neel reports that many sittings began, as is common in Native society, by establishing ties of affinity and descent between the sitter and the photographer. ¶ Neel says that being with these Native chiefs and elders changed the way he works as a commercial photographer. In Dallas he had learned what he calls a 'slick' style from other photographers with whom he worked. He calls adopting this style 'putting on a mask,' and found that it was unnecessary with the Native sitters, who are 'real people,' 'approachable people.' People who 'know who they are,' people who carry names that originated in the myth time, people who live in the intimacy and connectedness of small villages, have no need to project or hide behind images or masks. Neel contrasts the stability of the Native world with the constantly changing world of the non-Native. This is especially evident in the different attitudes toward the old. The Native elder, who carries the orally transmitted

knowledge of his or her family, is respected for that knowledge as well as the wisdom acquired through living. In contrast, the aged in the non-Native world, where knowledge (or information) is constantly changing and the new is more highly valued than the old, are not respected for their age (although, of course, they may earn respect through achievement). ¶ Patterns of power in the two societies differ as well. In the Native world, especially in the coastal cultures, hereditary chiefs and high-ranking people are born into their positions and raised to be leaders from infancy. Who they are is known to everyone. In non-Native society power is a personal acquisition, and often a tenuous one, which must be continually affirmed and asserted – and worn like a mask. 'It's hard to know,' says Neel, the portrait photographer, 'where the image stops and the person begins.' ¶ So, being Native is not, as in the Western 'culture of imaging,' a matter of appearances, stereotypes, and props. It is a way of being and a matter of shared values: respect for the family, the old, and the land. Paradoxically, perhaps, being Native is also being highly individualized – personal differences are permitted to flourish in these communities, and personal space is respected by others, to a degree unrecognized by the Outsider culture. And it is as individuals, as people who know who they are, that the sitters in Neel's photographs look back at us.

BIBLIOGRAPHY

Introduction:

Andrews, Ralph W. 1962. *Curtis' Western Indians*. New York: Bonanza Books

Berger, John. 1972. *Ways of Seeing*. London: British Broadcasting Corporation and Penguin Books

Curtis-Graybill, Florence and Victor Boesen. 1976. *Edward Sheriff Curtis: Visions of a Vanishing Race*. New York: American Legacy Press

Davis, Barbara A. 1985. *Edward S. Curtis: The Life and Times of a Shadow Catcher*. San Francisco: Chronicle Books

Duff, Wilson. 1965. *The Indian History of British Columbia, Volume 1: Impact of the White Man*. Victoria: BC Provincial Museum

Hathaway, Nancy. 1990. *Native American Portraits*. San Francisco: Chronicle Books

Jonaitis, Aldona. 1988. *From the Land of the Totem Poles: The Northwest Coast Indian Art Collection at the American Museum of Natural History*. Vancouver: Douglas & McIntyre

King, J.C.H. 1979. *Portrait Masks from the Northwest Coast of America*. New York: Thames and Hudson

LaViolette, F.E. 1961. *The Struggle for Survival: Indian Cultures and the Protestant Ethic in British Columbia*. Toronto: University of Toronto Press

MacEachern, Chief Justice Alan. 1990. *Delgamuukw v. A.G. of BC: Reasons for Judgement*. BC Supreme Court

Neel, David. 1991. 'An Opportunity Missed.' *Vancouver Sun*, 19 April

Richardson-Fleming, Paula and Judith Luskey. 1986. *The North American Indians: In Early Photographs*. New York: Dorset

Schwartz, Joan M. 1981-2. 'The Past in Focus: Photography and British Columbia, 1858-1914.' *BC Studies* 52

Todd, Douglas. 1992. 'In the Planet's Court: Economy vs. Ecology.' *Vancouver Sun*, 18 January

Wyatt, Victoria. 1989. *Images from the Inside Passage: A Northern Portrait by Winter and Pond*. Vancouver: Douglas and McIntyre

Afterword:

Burgin, Victor. 1982. 'Introduction.' In Victor Burgin, ed., *Thinking Photography*, 1-14. Houndmills, Basingstoke, Hampshire, and London: Macmillan Education

Chalfen, Richard. 1984. 'Review of Frank Webster, *The New Photography*.' *Studies in Visual Communication* 10 (3):89-91

Clifford, James. 1988. 'Identity in Mashpee.' In James Clifford, *The Predicament of Culture*, 277-346. Cambridge and London: Harvard University Press

– and George Marcus, eds. 1986. *Writing Culture*. Berkeley: University of California Press

Hill, Rick. 1989. 'In Our Own Image: Stereotyped Images of Indians Leads to New Native Artform.' *Muse* 4 (4):32-43

Jacknis, Ira. 1984. 'Franz Boas and Photography.' *Studies in Visual Communication* 10 (1):2-60

Julien, Isaac and Kobena Mercer. 1988. 'Introduction – De Margin and De Centre.' *Screen* 29 (4):2-10

Lyman, Christopher M. 1982. *The Vanishing Race and Other Illusions: Photographs of Indians by Edward S. Curtis*. New York: Pantheon, in association with the Smithsonian Institution Press

Malmsheimer, Lonna M. 1985. '"Imitation White Man": Images of Transformation at the Carlisle Indian School.' *Studies in Visual Communication* 11 (4):54-75

Rosaldo, Renato. 1989. 'Imperialist Nostalgia.' In Renato Rosaldo, *Culture and Truth*, 68-87. Boston: Beacon

Ruby, Jay. 1981. 'Editor's Introduction to Photographs of the Peigan by Roland Reed (Photo Essay).' *Studies in Visual Communication* 7 (1):48-51

Scherer, Joanna Cohan. 1985. 'Review of Christopher M. Lyman, *The Vanishing Race and Other Illusions: Photographs of Indians by Edward S. Curtis*.' *Studies in Visual Communication* 11 (3):78-84

Schwartz, Joan M. 1982. 'The Past in Focus: Photography and British Columbia.' In Joan M. Schwartz, ed., *The Past in Focus: Photography and British Columbia, 1858-1914*, 5-15. A special issue of *BC Studies*, Number 52

Printed on acid-free paper ∞

Set in Cloister by George Vaitkunas
Printed and bound in Canada by D.W. Friesen & Sons Ltd.

Copy-editor and proofreader: Joanne Richardson
Book design: Robin Ward